KULESHOV ON FILM

KULESHOV ON FILM

WRITINGS BY LEV KULESHOV

Selected, translated and edited, with an introduction by
RONALD LEVACO
Film Department
San Francisco State University

UNIVERSITY OF CALIFORNIA PRESS
BERKELEY • LOS ANGELES • LONDON

University of California Press
Berkeley and Los Angeles, California

University of California Press, Ltd.
London, England

ISBN 0-520-02659-4
Library of Congress Catalog Card Number: 73-90666
Printed in the United States of America

FOR ROZLYN

CONTENTS

ACKNOWLEDGMENTS

THE PRESENT WORK is literally the result of a gift. Or perhaps it would be more accurate to say a series of gifts. Every writer who shares his life with other people—even if he is a scholar—knows about such gifts and generosity. Over the several years this project has been part of my life, I have been incalculably indebted to many generous people. I am only able to accord my thanks to some of them and, limited by space, unable fully enough to express my deepest gratitude to each of them.

In the beginning several people were crucial. My warmest thanks to Professor Peter Dart, University of Kansas, for turning over to me, his then graduate assistant, the single-copy photostats he had made of Lev Kuleshov's first book, so that, as he simply put it to me, "the thing could get done," while unflaggingly cheering me toward that end ever since. And, likewise, my special gratitude must go to Professor Steven Hill, University of Illinois, for his unhesitant bestowal on me of the most substantial Kuleshov materials and papers in his possession, which he had begun collating before I knew precisely why Kuleshov was significant.

Subsequently, there was a time during which the affectionate, unwavering confidence in my capabilities and efforts of two extraordinary teachers who became my friends, Professors John Fell, San Francisco State University, and Arthur Benavie, University of North Carolina at Chapel Hill, meant more to me than they know, because it exceeded my own confidence and because it showed me pleasure in my work.

For my introduction to phenomenology, structuralism, and semiology I have to thank especially Professor Thomas Pace, Southern Illinois University, and my then colleague and present friend, Professor Richard Lanigan, Chicago State University, with both of whom I sought to clarify the meaning and direction of my work. The unpretentious sharing of our work and their warmest comradeship became an indelible and compassionate example in pedagogical collectivism.

Clearly, in terms of my particular tutorial in Soviet studies and the Soviet cinema, I must express my deepest gratitude to Professor H. P. J. Marshall, Director, Center for Soviet Studies in the Performing Arts, Southern Illinois University, under whose unique auspices and remarkable tutelage my research was unfettered, supported, and directed.

Abroad, a number of research institutions and their representatives assisted me in my research. Not the least of these are the Inter-University Committee on Travel Grants and the International Research and Exchanges Board, indispensable past and present organizations that award and administer grants to American scholars named to the U.S.A.-U.S.S.R. exchange. Additionally, I must extend my gratitude to Marie Merson, Cinémathèque Française; Penelope Houston and Sam Rohdie, editors of *Sight and Sound* and *Screen*, respectively, at the British Film Institute; and in the Soviet Union, Isabella Epshtein at the Union of Soviet Cinematographers, Professor Ilya Vaisfeld, Lilya Mamantova, Yuri Slavich, and Professor Vladimir Utilov, all at VGIK, The All-Union State Institute of Cinematography, Moscow—and, of course, most particularly, the inimitable Alexandra Sergeevna Khokhlova.

I should also like to accord special thanks to Professor Jay Leyda and Mr. Ernest Callenbach, both of whom read the manuscript with patience and thoroughness and offered precise and clarifying criticism that turned my writing and translation in the direction of lucidity and parsimony—goals Kuleshov would have admired and which I hope, in some measure, to have achieved.

Finally, I wish to express my very personal thanks to my former wife, June Land Kirk, who unstintingly assisted in this work and who cared about it in more ways than I could ever acknowledge; to Vivienne Martin who endured, shared, and even celebrated the mysterious concerns and misadventures occasioned during my London tenure; and to Rozlyn Middleman Lash, who received the culmination of this twice-born project, badly dog-eared and dangerously derelict by the time she saw it, with grace, wisdom, and, as befits her nature, love, self-possession, and generosity.

London, San Francisco
May, 1974

INTRODUCTION

I

THE DISTINGUISHED and enduring fifty-year career of Lev Kuleshov virtually spans the history of the Russian and Soviet film. Landmark theoretician, director, professor at VGIK, Moscow's All-Union Institute of Cinematography, the successes and failures of Kuleshov's life reflect the very ethos of the Soviet cinema. Yet, with few of his films shown in the West, and his several books and scores of articles untranslated into English until this work, Kuleshov remains for us a shadowy background figure, an early experimenter trapped somewhere in the first chapters of film history.

In fact, Kuleshov was the first aesthetic theorist of the cinema. In the introduction to his first book *Art of the Cinema*, published in 1929, a group of his disciples—among them Vsevolod Pudovkin—had written no less a tribute than: "We make films—Kuleshov made cinematography." Indeed, Kuleshov estimated that over half the Soviet directors since 1920 had been his pupils, including most notably Pudovkin, Eisenstein, Barnet, Kalotozov, and, more recently, Parajanov. Thus, Kuleshov's influental, many-sided career invites much wider attention and closer examination.

When I arrived in Moscow in late March of 1970 to complete my research on Kuleshov, the city's streets still bore the traces of a hard and icy winter. Mild, spring-like weather was spreading northward over Central Europe, but here there were still gusts of the penetrating winter wind that I remembered was especially difficult for Kuleshov to endure. In letters to America (to Professor Steven Hill) Kuleshov had sadly written about his susceptibility to the piercing draughts in the halls of VGIK, where he had lectured now for some twenty-five years. I knew that each of the last successive winters Kuleshov had suffered from what appeared to be a chronic respiratory illness. What I did not know was that Kuleshov, seventy-one, and a heavy smoker, had also been suffering for some time from lung cancer, and that at the age of seventy-one he had died the day before my arrival.

For me, the trip to Moscow to meet Kuleshov was to have been the culmination of my research into his theories and my translation of his writings. The subsequent few days were a somber and unreal flurry of events: witnessing a most moving ceremony at Dom Kino, home of the Union of Soviet Cinematographers; attendance at Kuleshov's funeral; a warm meeting, first with his students and colleagues at VGIK and then with his widow, Alexandra Khokhlova. Khokhlova, possibly a few years Kuleshov's senior, had been not only his constant companion throughout his career but also the principal actress in most of his films, as well as his production assistant.

In the main hall of Dom Kino, Kuleshov lay in state in an open coffin on a bier overlaid with flowers, while for several hours hundreds of people filed by. I was later told that the mourners consisted of virtually the entire membership of the Soviet film world. I remember a rare appearance by Lily Brik (Mayakovsky's mistress and the widow of Osip Brik, the literary critic and member of the Formalist circle, who had co-written one of Kuleshov's screenplays), a pale, ephemeral figure, starkly clad in black caftan and slacks, whose vividly red-dyed hair gave her a resemblance to Khokhlova. At Khokhlva's side much of the time was Pyotr Galadzhev, one of the last survivors of the original Kuleshov Workshop. (The other, Leonid Obolensky, had been unable to travel from the Urals where he is a television director.) It was mentioned to me that Viktor Shklovsky, considered by many the doyen of Soviet literary critics, an early Formalist, and coauthor with Kuleshov of two screenplays, was at Dom Kino that afternoon.

Kuleshov was buried toward evening on March 31, 1970, at Novodevicha Cemetery in a grave alongside Vladimir Mayakovsky. Novodevicha is the cemetery where Turgenev, Chekhov, and Gogol are buried, along with Russia's most distinguished artists, scientists, and statesmen. Here, after the last memorial tributes were spoken by Kuleshov's colleagues from VGIK, among them Romm and Gerasimov, the cover of the coffin was put into place. It remains difficult to forget the tall, gaunt figure of Khokhlova, so composed until that moment, suddenly straining towards some last something. The most palpable sensation was that, in a very large sense, the death of Kuleshov marked the end of the major epoch of Soviet cinematography.

Lev Vladimirovich Kuleshov was born on January 1, 1899, in Tambov, southeast of Moscow. The son of an artist, he became absorbed by drawing as a child. If childhood dreams and obsessions are ever indicative of the turns one's life takes, it may be significant that Kuleshov's artistic leanings were combined with a succession of such dreams of jobs, all of which involved an almost sensual fascination with machines. Though a child's fascination with machinery is hardly uncommon, it is curious that Kuleshov's childhood interests combined the mechanical and aesthetic sensibilities later recapitulated in his theory of film.

After his father's death in 1910, Kuleshov was brought to Moscow by his mother, and at fifteen enrolled in the School of Painting, Architecture and Sculpture, his intention being to become a painter. While at the school (where Mayakovsky also trained), his interests turned toward theater design; but by chance he secured a job instead at the Khanzhonkov film studio as a set designer for the then noted director, Evgeni Bauer.

This was in 1916, and although the cinema in Russia was flourishing and Kuleshov recalled his enjoyment in watching such stars as Asta Nielsen and Max Linder, he remembered feeling no abiding fascination with the film at first. Still, that year and the next found him designing settings for Bauer's *King of Paris* and nine other features, as well as starring in Bauer's *After Happiness.* Kuleshov's disastrous, unschooled experience with acting may well have influenced the theories he was later to evolve, for his attempt at a "naturalistic" performance seemed painfully ludicrous to him when he watched it on the screen. While working with Bauer, Kuleshov was introduced to and became impressed by what was then called "American montage"—the rapid cutting, frequent close-ups and parallel lines of action of American films, particularly Griffith's. When Bauer, to whom Kuleshov had grown devoted, died while shooting *After Happiness*, it fell to Kuleshov to complete the film; and afterward, though he recalled that work without Bauer became unfulfilling, he nonetheless pressed for a directorial assignment with the Khanzhonkov studio.

There, in 1917, he completed his first film, made in the style of short-shot, "American montage" (later to become the basis of what became internationally known as "Russian montage"), *Engineer Prite's Project.* Apparently shot just after the Revolution, *Prite* was a semi-detective, semi-propaganda film with an industrial theme. The plot was thin, but the surviving two reels reveal Kuleshov's early predilection for outdoor environments and his eye for composition and architecture. Kuleshov himself described *Prite* as the first Soviet film to be "constructed dynamically and editorially, with the use of close-ups." [1]

It was while shooting *Prite* that Kuleshov became aware of the first of several unique properties of montage which he was to describe in a succession of theoretical articles and books, beginning in 1917. What Kuleshov discovered was that it was possible to create, solely through montage, a cinematic terrain that existed nowhere in reality. As is often the case, the discovery came about quite accidentally when, missing some shots of his actors looking at electrical cables strung on poles, Kuleshov conjectured that the same effect could be achieved by splicing shots of actors looking off-camera with sepa-

[1] Steven P. Hill, "Kuleshov—Prophet without Honor?" *Film Culture*, No. 44 (Spring, 1967), p. 6.

rately taken shots of the row of poles. As the poles and the actors were in different parts of Moscow, Kuleshov decided to term the effect the "artificial landscape" (also known as "creative geography"); and although concepts such as these may seem ingenuous in retrospect, it is important to note that they had not yet been articulated, so far as is known, by anyone else.

The most diverse cross-currents characterized this period of Kuleshov's apprenticeship. The dynamism, eclecticism, and radicalism of the times were embodied in polemically combative avant-garde cliques such as the Constructivists, Futurists, and Formalists. At the same time, supporters of the Provisional Government sensed apocalypse hanging heavy in the air. In a culture that traditionally vibrated with occultism, the spirit of mediums like Mme Blavatsky, who had died some twenty years before, in part prefigured the mysticial extravagance and sensuality of composers like Scriabin, painters like Kandinsky, and maestros like Diaghilev. Apace with another current pervasive in Russia at the beginning of the century, Marxist artists with a Promethean vision of man's capability to transform his world began to see their art wedded to a new, social purpose.

And what about the "moving pictures" which it had been intellectually fashionable to deride before the Revolution? Avant-garde filmmakers harbored a vigorously expressed contempt for the socially purposeless aestheticism and theatricality of the "naturalistic" Moscow Art Theater, and for the potboilers of pre-Revolutionary cinema, the excesses of the melodramas, drawing room farces and romances which they saw as symptomatic of a decadent bourgeois sensibility. Committed to artistic innovation in which social consciousness was fused with their aesthetics, revolutionary artists began producing manifestos that audaciously represented the positions of their particular groups. Mayakovsky's "Theater, Cinema, Futurism," published in 1913, can be regarded as a precursor of what soon became a deluge of such manifestos. Groups like the Futurists were prepared to embrace the cinema as a mass art of unprecedented power; and in such a climate, the development of an aesthetic for the film could be an auspicious venture. It is ironic that the fierce exhortations for social commitment in the arts, which legitimized film as art in the Soviet state, also foreshadowed the very ideological tangles that enmeshed filmmakers like Kuleshov and Eisenstein during the thirties.

From the first, Kuleshov was absorbed by formal, structural problems. To some extent, he certainly benefited from the semiotic analyses of the early Formalists—the Petrograd Opoyaz and Moscow Linguistic Circle—who were developing a structuralist methology for dealing with literature as a system of signs. Some of the most prominent of the Formalists were to be quite active in film in later years. Among these, as has been mentioned, both Shklovsky and Brik were to collaborate on scripts with Kuleshov.

In theater circles, two representative currents of thought, which might shed additional light on the evolution of Kuleshov's work, emerged through essays espousing almost contrary positions (both published at about the same time in 1912–1913). Both positions were essentially classicist reactions to the excesses and decadence of the performing arts especially. The first was Leonid Andreyev's, the second Vsevolod Meyerhold's. Andreyev proposed that the way to a resucitation of spiritless theatrical forms was through concentration on the "inner soul drama" and the "extensions of the pan-psyche." He exhorted the theater to abandon activity, crowd movements, in fact all the "reproduction of visible, physical life," relegating them to the cinema where he felt them to belong.[2] Meyerhold, on the other hand, championed the return of the theater to more primitive actor-audience relationships, to the methods of the *commedia dell'arte* and the use of the actor's body as equivalent in expression to the spoken word.[3] For Kuleshov, the two positions were not mutually exclusive. As evidenced by his theoretical work and his most celebrated film, *By the Law,* he was to show a proclivity for both.

In both theory and practice, Kuleshov's own preferences inclined toward structural analysis: toward reduction, identification, and

[2] Jay Leyda, *Kino: A History of the Russian and Soviet Film* (George Allen and Unwin, London, 1960), pp. 56–57.

[3] *Ibid.,* p. 58.

interrelationship. He sought to identify the very "material" of the cinema and reasoned that it must be the celluloid itself, not the photographic image. As music was the manipulation and ordering of sounds, and painting the application and ordering of pigments, cinema was quintessentially the ordering of strips of film. For Kuleshov that was the *sine qua non*—what he termed the "filmness" of the cinema. Consistent with that line of reasoning, he announced audaciously that what was conventionally called the narrative or dramatic "content" of a film was irrelevant to the structuring of its "material." Accordingly, Kuleshov wrote in one of his earliest articles that the predetermined order in which pieces of film were joined—in other words, montage—was the irreducible source, the alpha and omega, of the cinematographic impact on the viewer, and he reiterated that how the shots were assembled was more important than what they were about.[4]

This provocative conclusion made it possible (indeed necessary) for Kuleshov to begin considering a whole series of problems concerning film acting—problems into which the Meyerholdian concept of the actor's body as a "word-equivalent" could be integrated. At the same time, Kuleshov defined the shot as a "shot-sign" which could be syntactically integrated, as a "word-equivalent," into a film comprised of other shots. From this followed the obvious analogy of (film) *sequence* and *sentence* (which Kuleshov used early on) and his subsequent, now infamous dictum that a film is built "brick by brick" (the repudiation of which Eisenstein swaggeringly handled in three or four short paragraphs of his essay "Za kadrom," published in 1929).

Kuleshov's searchings also led him to consider whether, under the powerful influence of montage, the spectator perceives an intentionally created *Gestalt* in which the relationship of shot to shot overrides the finer aspects of any actor's performance. The famous "Kuleshov effect" with the Russian actor Mozhukhin affirmed the speculation.

[4] Lev Kuleshov, *Iskusstvo Kino: Moi opyt* (Tea-Kino Pechat', Moscow, 1929), pp. 16–18.

Having found a long take in close-up of Mozhukhin's expressionlessly neutral face, Kuleshov intercut it with various shots, the exact content of which he himself forgot in later years—shots, according to Pudovkin, of a bowl of steaming soup, a woman in a coffin, and a child playing with a toy bear—and projected these to an audience which marveled at the sensitivity of the actor's range.[5]

During the next two years, 1919–1920, the outbreak of war between White and Red armies created a documentary theater and training ground for young Soviet artists. Penetrating the combat zones in agit-trains, filmmakers, poets, and artists (among them Dziga Vertov, Eisenstein and Mayakovsky) set out to polemicize the war. As an enviably experienced filmmaker, Kuleshov was able to shoot several short films (called *agitkas*—precursors of later, more developed forms of agit-prop), culminating in the unique two-reeler *On the Red Front.* Completed in 1920, *On the Red Front* was the first Soviet film to combine documentary footage with acted sequences.

Traveling between the front and Moscow during these years, Kuleshov found his intersts in film theory and pedagogy were unabated, and in 1919 he became active in organizing the first State Film School. That September, he began to conduct classes which led to the formation in 1920 of the Kuleshov Workshop. With the Workshop—it comprised, among others, Khokhlova, Pudovkin (seven years his teacher's senior), and, for a few months, Eisenstein—Kuleshov pursued experiments in montage. He created other "artificial landscapes" in which actors walked "towards" each other from different, distant sections of Moscow and suddenly met in a two-shot. He combined shots of the American White House with shots of the steps of a well-known Moscow building up which he had his actors walk, thus creating buildings and cities that existed only on the screen. He "synthesized" a woman filmically by combining separate shots of several women's bodies. In short, he sought to demonstrate that physical space and "real" time could be made virtually subordinate to montage.

[5] Vsevolod Pudovkin (Tr. Ivor Montagu), *Film Technique and Film Acting* (Vision, London, 1954), p. 140.

And he sought to prove, in turn, that the source of the associational power of montage was in the viewer's consciousness, his perception of the edited material, which did not necessarily bear any relationship to "objective reality." Such formalism was to prove heretical to the more truculent party ideologues, who saw in this preoccupation with form and structure the potential submergence of vital and "objective" themes and truths which it was imperative for the cinema to convey to the Soviet masses. For the zealous, twenty-one-year-old Kuleshov, however, the machinations of party judgment were a distant, perhaps as yet inaudible thunder.

Kuleshov was aware that his previous conclusions about the shot as "sign" required the formation of a rigorous course in which actors could learn to express themselves within what one Soviet critic called the sparse, laconic and unambiguous shots into which his style of cinema was evolving.[6] Presaging the use of actors by such modern directors as Bresson, Antonioni, and Resnais, the Kuleshov method sought to clarify and externalize the actor's emotions before the camera, to systematize and virtually to codify his use of physiognomy and gesture to express specific emotional states. This entailed a Meyerholdian emphasis on gesture and the grotesque combined with the pseudoscientific studies of bodily expression by the nineteenth-century Frenchman François Delsarte, whom Kuleshov was then studying (and from whom Eisenstein possibly derived his concept of "typage").

Kuleshov began to term his actors "models" and to regard them practically as mannequins. He demanded of them the most arduous physical preparation and the ability to perform any trick, any movement of the body, hands or legs.[7] This use of actors was then enhanced by placing them in contexts with fairly prominent, carefully chosen objects that would convey character traits or moods. In *Your Acquaintance* (also *The Female Journalist*) (1927), for example, Kuleshov was to use an absurd glass elephant on a wall shelf and a coat

[6] N. Zorkaya, *Portrety* (Moscow, 1966), p. 18. (my translation)
[7] *Ibid.*, p. 20

hanger thrust into a vase to evoke what he felt to be the essence of the room and its resident. He termed such objects "curiosities." But what he sought to develop was a primitive cinematic iconology.

By 1920 Kuleshov's group had begun to work on exercises that evolved into what came to be known as the "films without film." Reconciling themselves to dire shortages of film stock, the Workshop took up the construction of études, which were performed before an unloaded camera. (In principle, this sytem was carried over to VGIK where, with modifications, it is still used.) To assist his student-actors, Kuleshov conceived the cinematic space as analogous to a pyramid resting on its side, the base of which would be the rectangular screen. To assess composition and facilitate the plotting of movement, he went so far as to describe the space in graphic terms as a three-dimensional "metric web" formed by a net of horizontal and vertical lines (like graph paper, only projected into three-dimensional space). Thus, within this solid geometric space, any movement or shape could be explicitly mapped, described, and analyzed. What Kuleshov failed to describe explicitly was how this topological notation could be handled. Nonetheless, speculating that because the predictable lines and angles of industrial architecture were more distinct on the screen than, say, an ornate shot of a rural village, Kuleshov used the concept of the "metric web" to conclude (it would seem speciously) that the strongest line or movement on the screen would fall along one of the horizontal or vertical lines of the "web," and would thus be either parallel or perpendicular to the edges of the screen.

Despite such blind alleys, Kuleshov searched tirelessly for general laws governing the relationship of actor movement to cutting and composition. He strove to make his actors aware of *duration as movement*— a first principle of the cinema that is still valid, namely, that screen action always has to conform to the imperatives of cutting, to the montage of a particular sequence as conceived by the director, in order to be effectively locked into the structure of a film. Insofar as Kuleshov's intent was to create a director's cinema and to produce actors with a director's sensitivity, it is significant that several members of the Workshop—Khokhlova, Obolensky, Boris Barnet, and Pudovkin—went on to become directors. Needless to say, his system demanded scrupulous preplanning, which, according to its proponets, did allow for creative impulse and the luxury of errors—but in rehearsal rather than on film.

The "films without film" thus involved strict exercises in which the most seemingly basic and "natural" movements were systematically broken down to their most minute, irreducible components (perhaps suggestive of the linguist's approach to "ordinary" speech). Obviously this produced a spare, stylized aesthetic of acting, at best suited only for a silent cinema. Yet, ironically, even Kuleshov's silent films are characterized as much by the violation of his principles as by their observance; for his actor-training seemed to serve as the proverbial canon from which actors could diverge. At all events, Kuleshov's theories were, with little doubt, a pioneer attempt to come to grips, however primitively, with an acting "code" or method of expression for the screen: a foundation for a semiology of film acting, Shunning intuition and striving to arrest any tendency toward the then often hyperbolic style of Stanislavskian acting, Kuleshov admittedly created an ascetic style that his actors often transcended. What remains difficult, as always, is gauging the extent to which creative energy straining against the impositions of technique contributed to a successful result.

Having recruited a stock company composed of budding actors and ex-athletes, Kuleshov made, in 1924, a detective satire called *The Extraordinary Adventures of Mr. West in the Land of the Bolsheviks. Mr. West* served multiple purposes. First, it was (as *The Death Ray* was to be) a catalog of effects, and a means to show off the cinematic sophistication of the Workshop in its first big venture. Secondly, it was the first post-Revolutionary comedy in the Sennett style of the Americans, and came out during arduous years when the market for laughter was great and when Kuleshov wanted to demonstrate his ability to compete with Hollywood. Thirdly, it was at once a satire on the ludicrous preconceptions Americans ostensibly had about Soviet Russia and a parody of American detective thrillers. With its Harold Lloyd-like central figure (a senator and YMCA official who comes to

Russia to see it for himself), its episodic plot, and chases, *Mr. West* became an instant popular and critical success.

By 1925, Kuleshov, who had worked with Eisenstein on structuring crowd scenes, completed a sort of science fiction thriller called *The Death Ray.* Much more dramatically diffuse and thematically pedestrian than *Strike* (to which its crowd scenes have been unfavorably compared), *The Death Ray* was additionally encumbered by a tangled plot written by Pudovkin. It dealt with the theft of a secret laser-like ray, stolen from its Soviet inventor by a group of (prophetically conceived) Fascists, and its eventual recovery. Much less architectonic than *Strike,* the crowd sequences of *The Death Ray* had nonetheless (as perhaps their only virtue) a realistic, almost documentary appearance. Because they are not contained within the quadrate of the frame but consistently "spill over" and extend somewhere beyond it, the action of these sequences evokes the style of more recent films as Jancsó's *The Red and the White*, in which the camera attempts to perceive but not to impose form on the event.

The following year must have seemed an inauspicious one for Kuleshov. With *The Death Ray* under attack as neither economically nor ideologically justified, Kuleshov was on the verge of being dropped by his studio, Goskino.[8] After looking vainly for a lower-budget script to shoot, he set about adapting a story of Jack London's, "The Unexpected," with the collaboration of Viktor Shklovsky, and managed to complete the scenario in one night. The studio, Goskino (later Sovkino), accepted the script, and shooting began on what was to be Kuleshov's finest and most celebrated film.

By the Law (also known as *Dura Lex*) deals with the shattering effect of "the unexpected" on the minds of people whose lives are largely personally unexamined, canalized by tradition, and who govern themselves strictly by established ethical codes. Set almost entirely in a one-room cabin, the film makes no use of parallel lines of action and sustains an intensity that was achieved, in the words of the Soviet dramatist Tretyakov, "in the spirit of an algebraic

[8] Leyda, *Kino*, p. 212.

formula, seeking the maximum of effect with the minimum of effort." In a desolate region of the Yukon, during the Gold Rush, five prospectors share both the cabin and their claim. Suspecting the others of hatching a plot to make off with the whole stake, Michael Dennin guns down two of the plotters. Intent on upholding a semblance of legality, the other pair, Hans and Edith Nelson, feel obliged to try the murderer before they execute him. Performing a ritual trial made ludicrous by their circumstances, the Nelsons unremittingly exact their moral retribution, as Dennin's God-fearing, law-abiding peers. But their own tensions become unbearable. The grim dénouement is a hanged Dennin, a cataleptic Edith, and a brutalized Hans. Diverging from London's ending, in which Dennin dies on the rope, grotesquely dancing on the air, while a group of Indians watches uncomprehendingly from a clearing, the final sequences of the film show Dennin staggering from the hanging-tree to haunt the cabin, the frayed end of the broken rope still around his neck. In shock, unable within their own code of justice to hang the same man twice, the Nelsons are themselves condemned to living with their final memory of Dennin stumbling off through the incessant rain into the darkness of the night.

In his Workshop études, as in his previous films, Kuleshov had striven to choreograph and encode a kinesthetic drama for the screen, using both his "body language" acting system and his concept of montage as a system of "shot-signs." He thrust his actors into an overt dramatic world of somersaults, tricks, leaps, battles, and chases. He mistrusted the cinema's potential for depicting man's interior world; and, indeed, perhaps as some legacy of industrial mechanization, mistrusted the indulgence of any dramatic art that was preoccupied with the "interior." Now, the need to tackle the acutely psychological *By the Law* augured a reassessment. If Andreyev's exclusion of the cinema from the "inner-soul drama" was correct, *By the Law* would seem destined for disaster. On the other hand, if Kuleshov could penetrate the drama of Edith Nelson's struggle to resolve the tension of her doctrinal sense of justice versus her tortured compassion for Dennin, he should accomplish it using the very principles of film theory he had invested nearly ten years in formulating. What Kuleshov's success with *By the Law* affirmed was that montage, as the syntactic structure of film, dictates no imperatives, no textual substance of its own. It is the very structure of the cinema, the linguistic system as it were, the cinematic "code," which preexists, as Peter Wollen puts it, the "message" of any given film.[9] Through montage, Kuleshov could draw the viewer into the dramatic space in a way that conventional theater could not do. What remained was to lock the dramatic content into the montage, and Kuleshov accomplished this with some measure of success.

For example, in the execution sequence, the spasmodic movements of Khokhlova's rawboned arms—at once an affirmation toward heaven and an imprecation of her wretchedness—become physical analogues to the skeletal limbs of the twisted hanging-tree. The branches of the tree and Khokhlova's spindly arms, silhouetted in long-shot against an expanse of grey winter sky, with the horizon set almost at the bottom of the frame, evoke the terrible solitude of the marionette-like figures acting out their pantomime of justice in the vacuous space of the shot. Then, as Edith struggles to push the barrel from beneath Dennin's feet as he awaits his plunge to death, Kuleshov cuts to a close-up of her sliding feet as the traction, the grip on things which they seek, eludes them. A way of assessing the importance of montage in such a sequence is to consider, as Kuleshov does in his writing, the difference between the pro-filmic event and the edited sequence as it finally appears on the screen. Entirely consistent with the work of the Formalists and of his friend and co-scenarist (*By the Law* and *The Great Consoler*) Viktor Shklovsky, Kuleshov's conclusion is that the identification of the specific properties of montage lies in the difference between the phenomenal, presentational "reality" of the pro-filmic event before the camera, on the one hand, and the screen event, on the other. Thus, for Kuleshov, montage is the sum of all shooting and editing options exercised by the filmmaker.

[9] Peter Wollen, *Signs and Meaning in the Cinema* (University of Indiana Press, Bloomington, 1969), p. 117.

In *By the Law* Kuleshov also exercised some of those options early in the film. A sequence like the following can create an air of tension through the alternation of shots with intentionally unsteady and unstable compositions: one lone pine tree is shown momentarily; then the wind-blown hair of Edith Nelson; then the wind whipping the corner of a canvas tent. People's movements are sudden and jerky. The contrast of black-clad figures is emphatic against the snow. Here, what was absent in Kuleshov's earlier films—a sense of mood—pervades the film.

What Kuleshov evolved in *By the Law* was an adaptation of his earlier, more ascetic and mechanistic concepts, now applied to a cinema of microcosm, a cinema of precisely the kind of "inner-soul drama" that Andreyev had reserved for the theater. To do so (much as Room did the following year in the remarkable *Bed and Sofa*), Kuleshov had to move his camera to work from "inside" the film, as it were, to probe his characters more intensely than any Soviet film had done. Because the film seemed a reversion to the psychologism Kuleshov earlier decried, *By the Law* was stormily received by many Soviet critics. For some the film lacked ideological attack. For others it was simply too morbid. In an era of Soviet filmmaking which inspired Moussinac's "Un film d'Eisenstein ressemble à un cri, un film de Poudovkine évoque un chant," [10] Kuleshov's film seemed rather to engender a dirge.

For Kuleshov the director, this was the beginning of a period of failure, struggle, and eventual ideological recantation. His subsequent three silent features, *Your Acquaintance* (also called The Female Journalist, 1927), *The Gay Canary* (1929), and *The Great Buldis* (1930), were all unsuccessful. None of them a film with an inspiring revolutionary theme, they must have seemed all the more dismal and confusing to Soviet audiences by comparison with their contemporaries, *The End of St. Petersburg, October,* or *Arsenal.* Kuelshov's flagging spirits and his reputation only partially upheld by the publication in 1929 of his first major theoretical work, *Art of the*

[10] *Ibid.,* p. 221

Cinema (originally entitled *A Grammar of Film Art*), Kuleshov continued working on several documentary and information films. During the next few years, having transferred to another studio, probably under duress, Kuleshov also found himself burdened with the studio bosses' rejection of Khokhlova as simply not "box-office." It was decidedly a period of eclipse.

In 1932, again with the collaboration of Shklovsky (and G. Mundblit), Kuleshov wrote the scenario for a film he called *Horizon*, about a Russian Jew's emigration to the United States during the period of the pogroms, his devastating disillusionment there, and eventual return to his now Soviet motherland. Gamely, Kuleshov faced the transition to sound, struggling to bring to it the same demands for verisimilitude that had been his hallmark in the silent cinema. In *Horizon* there was no instance of off-camera music that was not motivated by the story; what seemed for an instant like background music would be revealed as coming from, say, a garden orchestra or an upstairs piano. Moreover, Kuleshov paid scrupulous attention to sound perspective—the quality of sound at a distance—rather than merely to its volume. That, and *Horizon's* rather accurate depiction of the desolation of urban America (gleaned largely from American films) made Kuleshov's first venture into sound cinema uncommonly modern.

Still, his excessively static camera, silent-film aesthetics of montage looked antiquated when grafted on to a sound cinema in which dialogue made longer takes necessary. In *Horizon,* shots of short duration and static composition simply became dreary. The sense of what a Soviet critic has called a sort of despondency or vacuousness characteristic of the Kuleshovian shot, and so expressive in the silents, when juxtaposed against longer dialogue-filled sequences became simply too plaintive and sentimental.[11] With actors the situation was even worse. Having become used to demonstrating a single, unambiguous emotion in a short montage shot, actors now provided with text and dialogue, and stuck before a camera for necessarily longer takes,

[11] Zorkaya, *Portrety*, pp. 38–39. (my translation)

seemed lifelessly wooden. This problem was accentuated by the declamatory training most Russian actors then received, especially from Kuleshov's bane, Stanislavsky's Moscow Art Theater.

All these difficulties were still to beleaguer Kuleshov in his next film, the final one within the scope of interest in this introduction. *The Great Consoler* (1933) seems to me the film in which a weary and assailed Kuleshov attempted to pose his own dilemma as a Soviet artist. During the late twenties and early thirties, a number of incidents cast a pall over the Soviet film world—as, indeed, over all the arts. The suicides of Esenin in 1925 and Mayakovsky in 1930, the collapse of such spirited avant-garde movements as LEF (The Left Front in Literature), the abolition of all private printing at the close of the period of the NEP, and Stalin's demand before the Sixteenth Party Congress for greater control over the arts, all portended the period of terror and the purges of the next two decades. Long before the official invocation of socialist realism in 1934, Abram Moiseevich Deborin, the editor of the leading philosophical journal of the time, *Under the Banner of Marixism,* had argued that art could only be transformed by profound social and economic change, and that therefore no non-socialist culture could precede and serve the imperatives of a new proletarian society. Deborin's was essentially a classical Marx-Bukharin interpretation of the relationship of art to culture and politics, and it is echoed by Kuleshov himself in a section of his essay "The Film Today" (1925), which is translated and included in the present work. But by 1925, the formation of the reactionary Association of Proletarian Writers (RAPP) and its filmworkers equivalent (ARRK) made it clear that Deborin's warning was to go unheeded. The transformation of the arts into a service industry and of the artist into a cadre had begun.

Kuleshov's *The Great Consoler* was released in the thick of the wranglings that culminated in the official adoption of socialist realism by the Congress of Soviet Writers in 1934. Loosely based on the period in prison of William Sydney Porter (O. Henry), the film took up the question of a writer's responsibility to represent reality as he knows it, without amelioration, for the presumably sensitive reader, and thus possibly to reinforce the reader's suffering. The film operated on multiple levels, mixing illusion and reality, interweaving biographical material from Porter's time in an Ohio penitentiary with segments from his stories.

In Kuleshov's film, Porter spends his time in prison talking with one of his own fictional characters, the safecracker Jimmy Valentine. Racked by tuberculosis, Valentine is heartened by one of Porter's stories in which he sees himself depicted as a dapper, elegant hero, and, by succumbing to wish-fulfilling fantasies instead of struggling for a redress of his grievances with a brutal judicial system, is rendered utterly impotent. Dissolving to a dream sequence, Kuleshov shows us a graceful, healthy Valentine using his skills to crack a safe in which a little girl is trapped. He becomes the town hero and, as is the custom, marries the pretty lady who gratuitously happens to be the child's aunt. Then, there is an abrupt shift to "reality." Valentine is dragged out of prison and coerced to free the little girl by false promises of clemency. In drab prison garb, on the verge of death, his talents as a safecracker are exploited; after the rescue, his sandpapered fingertips bleeding, he is taken back to prison to die in ignominy. Meanwhile, Porter is rewarded by the authorities for his exemplary docility—he is given books and paper and made a trusty.

We cut to another level of the narrative. The shopgirl Dulcey (Khokhlova) also "loses herself" in O. Henry's fiction to escape the desolation of her life. But, compromised by a seedy detective, Ben Price, to whose seduction she succumbs out of poverty and loneliness, it is Dulcey who finally rejects the rose-tinted world of her "consoler," O. Henry, and rises up against Price to shoot him. Ruin all around him, Porter realizes too late the polemical power of the pen, which he might have used toward altering the repressive social order he cajoled his readers into accepting.

Technically, *The Great Consoler* suffered from some glaring shortcomings. The rather complex structure of the narrative was not well handled, which made transitions awkward and advanced the plot so unevenly that the "shape" of the film suffered. Kuleshov was further hampered by the primitive quality of Soviet film stock (this was the first time domestic Soviet stock was used for a sound feature), and any further effects with sound beyond those initiated in *Horizon* were impossible. The sound quality was, in fact, poorer than in *Horizon.* Encumbered with Khokhlova's former husband as O. Henry, Kuleshov also had to contend with affected, bombastic playing by Konstantin Khokhlov of Stanislavsky's M.A.T. But despite these difficulties, even despite what might appear a banal subject for the Western viewer, *The Great Consoler* strikes me as Kuleshov's most profound film. And ironically, on a level that apparently eluded the party critics who assailed him, it attested to his unwavering Marxism.

As Kuleshov conceived it, *The Great Consoler* was informed by the Marxist argument that art cannot exist free of its social context, that any fiction is embedded in a given milieu, which necessarily makes it an expression of social ideology. To the extent that the film at once parodied and denounced the counterfeit heroics of American films (as in the dream sequence in which Valentine rescues the child and gets the girl), neither O. Henry's stories nor American films often represented suffering as the degradation of people victimized by social systems. Rather, they usually chose to portray suffering as a way-station in the hero's quest to overcome adversity (often gratuitously) and so affirmed the predominance of "good" over "evil." That was perhaps the most common permutation of the Hollywood ending. In the context of Soviet revolutionary thought, any film which betrayed the socioideological matrix in which it was produced, which was not devoted to the betterment of man within the social context but was rather a function of the director's special interests, was presumed to indulge in the luxury of decadence or narcissism. It placed individual interest above the collective need. Moreover, nihilism in the Soviet film could be depicted as an assault on human fulfillment, but to have portrayed it as an ultimate human condition was to presume an elitist omniscience which by definition impoverished humanity and deterministically alienated the artist from the people.

This ideological framework became the crux of the distinction to be made between the "American" ending of *By the Law* and the Soviet one. Implicit in the London story (and in the English subtitles on the U.S. print) is an ending which turned on a cruel irony: the senselessness of the Nelsons' retributive style of justice. In London's story the motive for Dennin's action was unclear. However, Kuleshov's film saw the entire group victimized by "gold fever"—an obsessive, bourgeois drive towards amassing individual wealth—and hence as destroyed by its inevitable concomitants of greed and expediency. As a Marxist film, *By the Law* was more a microcosmic and materialist study of the futility of self-aggrandizement than a tragedy in which Dennin's suspicion and greed impelled him towards mayhem.

Similarly, *The Great Consoler* was a film which posed a question about the inherent social obligations of making films. At first glance, Kuleshov's question was whether the artist, in this case O. Henry, abetted the social system that oppressed him, his fellow convicts, and his readers by mollifying the direness of their plight. But the shadow question that emerged by implication was a far more perilous one for the times—whether a severely repressed society needed panegyrics to Stalinism or a depiction of the grim "reality" the artist saw. For just as Kuleshov's film represented Porter as having abdicated responsibility by creating his "beautiful lies," it also implicated all Soviet artists who bent to Stalin's yoke, including, as he must have realized, Kuleshov himself.

In the midst of all the critical controversy surrounding *The Great Consoler*, it was unlikely that Kuleshov could have miscalculated the extent of the slander that was to be heaped on him when the Congress of Film Workers convened in January 1935. The year after the film's release, Kuleshov had resolutely gone on to supervise one of his former students and longtime friends, Leonid Obolensky, in his direction of a film called *The Theft of Sight.* This, along with *The Great Consoler,* precipitated the denunciation of Kuleshov by members of the 1935 Congress, and his notably brief and remarkably unrepentant "confession" to formalistic errors, to having asserted the preeminence of form over content, and to having made "bad" films. Kuleshov's directorial career was doomed. He was never to direct another major film. He did, however, go on to make several anodyne films for children, one of which especially evidenced the unrelenting pressures of Stalinsim. Titled *The Siberians* (1940), it followed the exploits of two boys determined to return a lost pipe of Stalin's to its owner, who was portrayed, as was obligatory, as a benign, avuncular figure to whom all children instinctively gravitated.[12]

Kuleshov published six more books and booklets, the most substantial, apart from *Art of the Cinema* (1929), being his *Practice of Film Direction* (1935) and his massive practical textbook *Fundamentals of Film Direction* (1941). At present his memoirs, *Fifty Years*, jointly written with Khokhlova, await posthumous publication in Moscow. In 1944 despite his "formalist transgressions" Kuleshov was appointed Head of the Film Institute, largely through the efforts of Eisenstein, who joined him on the faculty of direction. In 1947 he was awarded his doctorate of arts and in 1967 he was fully "rehabilitated" with the most distinguished award his country bestows, the Order of Lenin. He continued, usually with Khokhlova, to lecture regularly at the Film Institute almost until his death on March 29, 1970.

II

In the eyes of the Stalinist critics who censured him as a Formalist in 1935, Kuleshov's crucial error (as revealed in his "confession" translated in this collection) lay in the early polemical position that the structuring of cinematic material—montage—overrode the significance of the narrative or dramatic events to be expressed. This was clearly a position informed by the early hypothesis of the Formalist group, Opoyaz (The Society for the Study of Poetic Language, founded in Petrograd in 1915 by Viktor Shklovsky and Boris

[12] Despite its obligatory homage to Stalin, *The Siberians* effectively marked the end of Kuleshov's directorial career; although he made three more children's films, Kuleshov decided to devote himself entirely to teaching cinema at VGIK, The All-Union State Institute of Cinematography in Moscow.

Eichenbaum, among others) that the true material of literature was language,[13] rather than plots, characterizations, or themes.

The genesis and history of the prevailing Stalinist attitudes in the 1930's toward literature and cinema, to which Kuleshov fell victim, is sufficiently complex to warrant clarification. For example, the glib attribution to Stalin and Zhdanov alone of the "narrowness" and "philistinism" officially expressed in the Soviet Union toward artistic experimentation (Zhdanov was Stalin's principal henchman in matters of censorship from 1934 onward and the Secretary of the Central Committee of the CPSU) today seems simplistic. Clearly, during the 1930's, it was Zhdanov's principal concern, under Stalin's directives, to "normalize" film and literature, to "bulwark art against the impingement of irrationality." [14] However, with his own suspicions of experimental art considered, what seems painfully apparent now is the extent of Lenin's complicity in this direction—a direction of censorship that led to an unprecedented suppression of artists in this century, a suppression that betrayed the theoretical principles not only of Kulesov, but also of Pudovkin, Eisenstein, Dovzhenko, and Vertov.

Since it was in these earlier ideological, critical, and aesthetic controversies, culminating in the official adoption of socialist realism in 1932 and the attendant purges and liquidations, that Lev Kuleshov became enmeshed, it would be well to determine the origins of the "problem" of Formalism, to ascertain what went wrong during the most promising epoch of Soviet cinema and the arts, and to ask what can be learned more generally about the conflict between artists and the State—a conflict not exclusive to the case of the USSR, but one which continues there to the present day.

To begin, a clarification of the background of artistic "transgression," as conceived under Stalin, seems illuminating and necessary. Three divisions of the origins of Stalinist-Zhdanovist suppression can

[13] Krystyna Pomorska, *Russian Formalism Theory and Its Poetic Ambiance* (Mouton, The Hague, 1968), p. 23.

[14] Maynard Solomon (Ed.), *Marxism and Art* (Alfred A. Knopf, New York, 1973), pp. 202–204.

be made: (1) pre-Leninist polemical controversies over the nature of art, literature, and the cinema, in which the Formalists played a leading and decisive role, during the years 1914–1917; (2) Lenin's own stated dispositions and attitudes toward art; and (3) the specific character of Zhdanovist objections to what were considered the prevailing "aberrant" tendencies in the Soviet arts of the Stalinist period of the late 1920's and early 1930's and their specific remedies, proposed by Zhdanov, in the context of his address to the Congress of Soviet Writers and the Soviet Union's official adoption of socialist realism in 1934.

Closely connected with the Futurist and Cubist movements of the 1910's through its aims to create new modes of aesthetic perception (and analysis, in the case of the Formalists) by derogating, "dismantling", and reconstructing traditional forms of art, the Formalists organized by 1915 to analyze "the (established) laws of literary production." [15] In this measure, although they were censured by doctrinaire socialist colleagues in the 1930's, both the Futurists and the Formalists should be located squarely and inventively in the tradition of the materialist analysis of art, since it was their intention, by identifying the rules of, say, the production of pre-socialist narrative, to augur its transformation by socialist artists and theorists. Moreover, it was the intent of the Formalists, as an enumeration of their methodology will reveal, to repudiate and invalidate traditional (and from their viewpoint static, retrograde, and non-dialectical) "interpretive," historical, and biographical criticism that dealt more with extraliterary questions (under the guise of what is still termed "criticism" in many academic circles). In short, as they proposed it, the Formalists' purpose was to provide a basis for a scientific, materialist, and, as will be shown, structuralist analysis of literature and cinema as systems of signs,[16] and thereby to create scientific theories of poetry, of prose, of cinema, and potentially of all the arts.

The Formalists sought first to understand and to disclose what

[15] *Ibid.*, p. 203

[16] See esp. Ch. 1, "The Formalist Theory of Poetic Language," in Pomorska, *Russian Formalist Theory and Its Poetic Ambiance.*

literature and cinema were considered by their audience to be—to understand how art was understood—before they broached the eminently more complex and necessary sociological and political questions that dealt with what the function of literature and cinema was to be. That the Formalists had been moving toward a "critical synthesis" of both questions was recognized by Bukharin as late as 1934 when he read a speech reintroducing Formalist concepts into the aesthetic field from which they had been proscribed since 1929. However, it was at this very Congress of Soviet Writers[17] that Zhdanov delivered the opening address officially invoking socialist realism as the policy of artistic creation and criticism that would eliminate decadent experimentalism, pornography, and other eccentric excesses produced by overzealous artists in the name of stylistic innovation, but out of contact with the unpretentiously "normal" preoccupations of the Soviet public. Bukharin was executed not four years later in 1938.

A closer examination of the principal components of the Formalist analysis of literary discourse proposed during the pre-Leninist period of 1914–1917 clarifies the nature of the ideological conflict and state repression that ensued. First, heavily influenced by early- and mid-nineteenth century dialectological and ethnographic studies of folklore and literature, the Formalists sought to create an anlysis that focused on the *style* and recurrent *conventions* of art.[18] Second, in the tradition of the outstanding Ukranian philologist, Aleksandr Potebnya (1835–1891), the Formalists drew sharp distinctions between *poetic* and *practical* (prosaic) language, and a complementary differentiation between *oral* and *written* style. Adapting a method from the eminent Polish linguist, Jan Baudouin de Courtnay (who heavily influenced the founder of modern semiology, Ferdinand de Saussure), the Formalists developed a system of comparison between oral and written style that they hoped, by a process of the elimination of paired, homologous elements shared by the two (which could then be

[17] Solomon (Ed.), *Marxism and Art*, pp. 202–204.
[18] Pomorska, *Russian Formalist Theory and Its Poetic Ambiance*, p. 15.

discarded as features *not* unique to *written* style) would leave them with the invariable constituent features of written style, features that existed uniquely in the written discourse that literate man termed "literature." [19]

Third, adopting the phenomenological Husserlian search for "essences" (Husserl's *Logische Untersuchuungen* had been translated and published in Russian in 1912), the Formalists sought to locate and name the *immutable,* essential stylistic elements of literary discourse by means of comparative studies of pronunciation and phonology, in which the elements of every message, be it oral or written, that are constant and unchangeable are separated from those that are variable, unsteady, and dictated by the fluctuations of, say, emotion in the process of speaking.[20] Fourth, the Formalists expressed the conviction that all human expression is part of a *system of values* established by a given culture, by means of communicating through, and making choices within, a system of signs, each of which has its own distinct existence in the sense that the system contains within itself signs and symbols that can be studied without reference to any originative, outside "referential" phenomena in nature.[21] Fifth, the Formalist studies, therefore, focused on the artistic text as the conjuncture of unique stylistic elements that constituted its "literariness" (and, in the case of film, what Kuleshov called its "filmness"), on the one hand; and the system of signs as inherently expressing social, conventional human values, on the other hand.[22]

Sixth, the Formalists thus focused on the artistic *product* (text), not process (biography, history, etc.); and, hence, biographical and historical information (which characterized much of nineteenth- and twentieth-century literary criticism) was suspended as irrelevant, since both the *material* and the *value systems* of artistic discourse were taken to reside in the structure—the *selection, organization,* and *assemblage* of signs—of the art work itself.[23] Seventh, the surface, overt, or

[19] *Ibid.*, pp. 16–18.
[20] *Ibid.*, p. 18.
[21] *Ibid.*, pp. 18–19.
[22] *Ibid.*, pp. 19–20.
[23] *Ibid.*, pp. 22–23

"presented" level (what is today often termed the "naive text") of any art work, was likewise suspended, in favor of an analysis of the structure—of the *choices,* the *organization,* and the *interrelationship* of the signs of expression, which were taken to be "psychic by nature," that is, having their origin in the human psyche. Thus, any such structural, semiotic study of the text alone would ineluctably embrace the study of cultural values and processes of cultural signification.[24]

Eighth, and finally, the Formalists thus concluded that language is "concrete by nature," because its signs constitute meaningful "associations ratified by the collective agreement" of the speakers within the language group (if you will, the people, the masses), and that these associations "are realities which have their seat in the brain," as Saussure himself had written. Thus, there is little question that the Formalists perceived their analytic methodology as both *materialist* and *mass oriented,* because language signs were taken *not* as "mere reflections" of an external reality but as concrete in themselves, and because language is a "mass medium" by definition.[25]

Hence, Kuleshov's film theory, his montage experiments, and his polemic advancing of the "primacy of the celluloid" itself as the true "material" of cinema bore more than a rudimentary resemblance to the Formalist approach. Furthermore, Kuleshov eclectically shared with the Futurists and Constructivists a fascination for the new (the futuristic), the mechanical, and the technological, as has been noted. Also, like many European avant-gardists, Kuleshov was hopeful of de-romanticizing, de-psychologizing, and de-bourgeoisifying the imagery of art, its structures and forms of narration, and the perceptual processes that traditionally often canalized its creation and conventionalized both its apprehension and appreciation. Even somewhat like Vertov, with whom he both worked and irremedially disagreed, Kuleshov hoped to create a cinematic montage that could transform and liberate the cinema from being mere "copy images," in the deterministically naturalist and realist traditions of the bourgeois

[24] *Ibid.,* pp. 23–25.
[25] *Ibid.,* pp. 26–27.

theater, on the one hand; and the equally deterministic "slices of life," "windows on the world," and "psychological interiorizations" of the bourgeois realist novel, on the other hand. Instead, like Eisenstein and under the influence of Meyerhold, as mentioned earlier, Kuleshov favored applying the dynamics of montage and the system of bio-mechanics to achieve his break with the traditional theater and novel. Hardly a scholar of philosophy, philology, or Formalism, Kuleshov sought, nonetheless, to approach cinema in ways often remarkably analogous to the Formalists'. But it was Kuleshov's futurist opposition to established genres and forms of expression and his perseverence in defining the very structure of cinematic expression in his theoretical writings for the apparent purpose not only of mastering the medium, but of freely choosing its organization and form in his filmmaking experiments that ultimately provoked the confusion and displeasure of the more aesthetically traditional and inflexible members of his audience—not the least of which might have been Lenin himself.

In order to understand the influence on Kuleshov of the Formalists' approach to language and art and to be prepared to understand the magnitude of the political tragedy and ideological inequity of his censure, ostensibly, along the lines of Marxist-Leninist principles, it is crucial to recognize that for the Formalists as for Kuleshov, the analysis of *the concreteness of the material of artistic discourse* rather than the traditional and equivocal, historical and social "interpretations" or "explications" of art (which paradoxically were and indeed still are mistaken for being more "objective" and "concrete") was entirely consistent with—indeed, derived from—the materialist interpretation of history.[26] Curiously, it was Lenin, himself, who ignored that Marx's materialism also included the production of human discourse, as the first thesis on Feurbach points out; but, instead, early felt that it lay, as Lenin put it, in the notion that "the real unity of the world consists in its materiality, that motion is the mode of existence

[26] See esp. Ch. 9, "Lenin's Philosophical Legacy," in Richard T. de George, *Patterns of Soviet Thought* (University of Michigan Press, Ann Arbor, 1970).

of matter, and that man is the product of nature and consciousness a product of the human brain." [27]

Lenin's personal dispositions and attitudes toward art can scarcely vitiate his political genius, but the canonical reverence in which he is often held—particularly by contrast with Stalin—need not prevent a critical examination especially of those of Lenin's attitudes and positions that bear on the question of the background of Soviet artistic repression. First, no less than Trotsky and Bukharin recalled that Lenin clearly regarded art as a mere substitute reality—and of an inferior order at that. A lover, as is known, of Beethoven's *Apassionata*, Lenin was dismayed, for instance, at the mysterious, uncontrollable origins and tenacity of his own unbounded aesthetic emotion, which he felt to displace and predominate over revolutionary activity, and was further convinced that creative life required a monetary and psychic extravagance, which he was not personally willing to countenance. Moreover, in the tradition of the most conventional nineteenth-century Russian critical thought, Lenin regarded art as a utilitarian vehicle of moral uplift, the principal function of which was to disseminate knowledge.[28] Lenin often equated "modernism" with decadence, feared the "chaos" of artistic experimentation, and held experimental art at a low social priority, as evidenced by his outrage at the publication in 1921 of Mayakovsky's revolutionary poem, "150,000,000." In fact, during the heated exchange of correspondence about it, Lenin angrily expressed his contempt for Futurism, which he felt should be "fought against"; for his sometime friend and colleague, Anatoli Lunacharsky, then Minister of Education (and, as such, also in charge of cinema), who authorized the publication of Mayakovsky and who he felt "should be whipped"; and for the poem itself, which he termed "pretentious trickery." [29]

Still, quarrels over the merits of Futurism notwithstanding, what remains both crucial and tragic is that it was a narrow and absolutistic

[27] *Ibid.*, p. 162.

[28] Solomon, *Marxism and Art*, pp. 166–167.

[29] Herbert Marshall (Ed. and Tr.), *Mayakovsky* (Hill and Wang, New York, 1965), pp. 30–32.

reading of the tenets of historical materialism that seemed to demand an adherence of an undistorted "realism" in art—a realism that "copied" nature manifestly for its audience; a realism that was thus destined as a "pseudo-nature"; and, finally, a realism that had to demonstrate its social utility as a mass medium of propaganda, while presumably leaving the perceptual processes and canalized aesthetic expectations of its audience intact. In fact, however, in Russia as in Central Europe, from the century's turn until shortly after the first decade of the Revolution, artistic experimentation in the direction of abstraction was not officially discouraged, for reasons perhaps more to do with decentralized "neglect" than design. For example, these years in the Soviet Union saw the emergence of the extraordinary constructions of Tatlin; the Cubo-Futurist posters of Rodchenko; Diaghilev's staging of Stravinsky's *The Rite of Spring*; Malevich's and Kandinsky's architectonic Suprematist and neo-symbolist paintings; Popova's astonishing settings for Meyerhold's production of *The Magnificent Cuckold*; indeed, the development of Meyerhold's system of the bio-mechanics of acting and movement in bodily expression itself.

Nonetheless, the origins of Soviet state discouragement and eventual censure and suppression of artistic experimentation "not reflective of reality" must also be seen to have its genesis in Lenin's early philosophical formulations and concerns, a particular examination of four elements of which attests the case: (1) Lenin's discussions of realism in *Materialism and Empirio-Criticism* (1908); (2) Lenin's "copy theory" of knowledge; (3) the function of pragmatism as a test of truth; and finally (4) Lenin's attitude toward "fantasy, falsification, and freedom of thought." [30]

In some of his fullest philosophical considerations of the nature of reality, Lenin begins by refuting the idealist attack against materialism, starting with George Berkeley in the eighteenth century. Like Engels, Lenin divides philosophy principally into two camps—the materialists, who hold that nature or matter are primary, and that

[30] de George, *Patterns in Soviet Thought*, p. 146–169.

mind is secondary; and the idealists, who hold that the reverse is the case.[31] Blurring the distinctions between "realism" and "materialism", Lenin rejects any realism that "oscillates" between idealism and realism as muddled. In his summary attacks against idealism, Lenin concludes that: (1) our sensations and consciousness are an image of the external world; (2) science attests the existence of the earth before man; (3) objects, things, bodies exist, therefore, outside man, and our perception consists of images of the external world; (4) since the world existed before society and the physical world does not depend on man to organize it (nature having its own manifest organization), it is matter that must be primary and not spirit; and (5) there must be objects, which we reflect, for there to be objective truth, and a denial of objects denies objective truth.[32]

This argumentation then permits Lenin to present his "copy" theory of knowledge. Put simply, Lenin contends, if the world exists independently of us, then consciousness is an image of the external world, and though sensation is admittedly subjective, its foundation, then, is objective. The relationship of the subjective and objective is therefore one of *correspondence*—that is, our ideas, derived from sensations, correspond to real objects around us. And thus, the "proper" use of our perceptions must be within prescribed limits to correspond with what we know to be the objective world.[33]

Since the function of human beings in the world depends in large measure on the accuracy of their perceptions, Lenin uses Engels to link the perception of reality with the question of social utility. For Lenin, as one might guess, if our knowledge were not true, if we did not adequately reflect the object, it would be impossible for us to use it successfully. Thus, for Lenin, the meaning of truth is pragmatic.[34] Some truths, of course, are not susceptible of direct observation but can be tested by coherence alone. For example, statements in the past such as "Caesar crossed the Rubicon," mean that there was a man

[31] *Ibid.*, p. 148.
[32] *Ibid.*, pp. 149–150.
[33] *Ibid.*, pp. 152–153.
[34] *Ibid.*, p. 156.

called Caesar who did cross the Rubicon, but to test the truth of this statement in the present, one would have to see how well it cohered or formed one piece with what we know of the past and present. Therefore, even intangible, past aspects of the objective world must conform to our sense of the present and the past with utility.[35]

Finally, with respect to fantasy and reality, Lenin warns that "it is possible for man to abstract incorrectly, to falsify, and to introduce freedom of thought or fancy."[36] It is decidedly this element of "fantasy" that is, for Lenin, "the source not only of error but also of fictions, and it is this, ultimately, which makes flights of fancy, false ideologies, and alienation possible."[37]

Consistent with his earlier reasoning in *Materialism and Empirio-Criticism* (1908), Lenin's specific attitudes toward artistic freedom and experimentation in art are significantly revealed in the following candid, personal observation, made by him in the early twenties:

> Every artist, and everybody who wishes to, can claim the right to create fully according to his ideal, whether it turns out good or not. And so you have the ferment, the experiment, the chaos. But, of course, we are Communists. We must not put our hands in our pockets and let chaos ferment as it pleases. We must consciously try to guide this developement, to form and determine its results. . . . We are good revolutionaries, but we feel obliged to point out that we stand at "the height of contemporary culture." I have the courage to show myself a "barbarian." I cannot value the works of expressionism, futurism, cubism, and the other *isms* as the highest expression of artistic genius. I don't understand them. They give me no pleasure.[38]

To fill the apparent need for an unequivocal approach to art that would end the experimentalist disputes and bring artistic endeavor in line with the conceptions and aims of state leadership, Josef Stalin officially invoked a state approach to art defined as socialist realism in the early thirties, namely, "the truthful, historically concrete presentation of reality in its revolutionary development which must be

[35] *Ibid.*
[36] *Ibid.*
[37] *Ibid.*
[38] Joseph Freeman *et al., Voices in October,* (NewYork, 1931), p. 55.

combined with the task of the ideological remaking and education of toilers in the spirit of socialism." [39] Thus, although its direction had been established under Lenin, the implementation of socialist realism was not advanced by Lenin but by Stalin, and policed by Andrei Zhdanov, from about 1932 until his own death in 1948. By 1934, speaking to the Union of Soviet Writers, Maxim Gorki elaborated the definition of socialist realism as having a function analogous to that of myth, which he conceived as fundamentally realistic, though having an exemplary component in which mythic heroes serve as models for emulation. Thus, Gorki's socialist realism is defined as "the embodiment of an imagining in an image," and, if to this one adds "the logic (or passion) of the possible wish (inherent in myth), mythic realism turns revolutionary." [40] And thus, Gorki sought to "have the kind of romanticism which underlies the myth, and is most beneficial in its promoting a revolutionary attitude toward reality, an attitude that in practice refashions the world." [41]

Though distinct from Stalin's definition, Gorki's was regrettably absorbed literally into it, as will become momentarily apparant, during the Zhdanovist period beginning in 1932, when Stalin had dissolved all previous writers' organizations, including RAPP, and consolidated his power over the literary and artistic community through the establishment of the present Union of Soviet Writers, ostensibly for the purpose of administering the problems and needs of Soviet writers more responsively. The indisputable decline of Soviet art, with the possible exception of the brief but unrealized liberalization during the "Thaw" in the mid-fifties, can be dated from that time (if not from 1927–28) to the present.

Unlike the positions of both the Formalists and of Lenin, the philosophical underpinnings of which have been educible in ideology, Zhdanovism seems to rest neither on any elaborated socialist methodology nor on philosophical premises, although from both the Zhdano-

[39] S. V. Utechin, *A Concise Encyclopaedia of Russia* (E. P. Dutton and Co., New York, 1964), pp. 499–500.

[40] Solomon, *Marxism and Art*, p. 242.

[41] *Ibid.*

vist propaganda writings and the evident conventionalization especially of narrative style and characterization (i.e., a retrograde change in the direction of nineteenth-century conventions, especially evident by contrast with the experimentalism in narrative style and characterization in these art forms during the twenties), one can extrapolate the "conditions" of Zhdanovism. First, Zhdanovism implied a rejection of complexity in art. Second, it fostered and encouraged a general desexualization of both life and the themes and imagery of art. Third, Zhdanovism would have the use of art, especially the cinema, be for the creation of an exemplary body of myths, celebrating Soviet life. Fourth, under Zhdanovism there was a general censorship of the arts by members of the state apparatus assigned (hence the attribution of the still derogatory Russian, *apparatchik,* to the bureaucrat who performs such a function) and the subjection of artists to what turned out to be repressive modes of state support and patronage by means of state subsidies to artists, which could be withheld at any juncture. Thus, the conditions under which many a youth worked, say, during the 1920's—as Kuleshov did when he founded what was in fact an independent experimental workshop—changed in the direction of centralized state control of, and disbursement for, all artistic production. Fifth, and last, Zhdanovism sounded a call for a kind of heroic self-portrature in especially the visual arts, accompanied by the perverse reasoning that if the bourgeois arts mirrored bourgeois decadence, then clearly the function of the Soviet arts in reflecting their "reality" must be to mirror "true" conditions—none of which conditions could possibly resemble the West's, since a revolution had been waged and an ideological structure erected to create a culture fundamentally different from decadent, bourgeois culture.[42]

However, what must also be added to the "conditions" of Zhdanovism were the actions, the behavior, the "living scenarios" that developed under Zhdanovism in film and theater circles beginning as early as 1927–28. It is the reflection of these events in the facts and

[42] *Ibid.,* pp. 235–241.

statistics of the Stalinist period that can more concretely inform and bear witness to the appalling victimization of Soviet film artists (indeed, all artists) during the twenty years that came to be known as the Zhdanovist period, until the death, first of Zhdanov in 1948, then of Stalin in 1953.

Beginning in 1924 with the death of Lenin, Stalin had assigned officials of the Party to administrative posts in the film industry, which led to its total ideological control.[43] At the same time, the number of studios was drastically cut and their administration centralized. Lenin had reinstituted censorship as early as 1922 (perhaps as a response to the otherwise "loosening" trend during the NEP), but these organizational shifts ensured it.[44]

By 1928, top-ranking officials of the Commisariat of Education, under whose aegis the cinema had been placed, decided to review the schedule of production for 1928 and banned thirty-six percent of the previously authorized scenarios.[45] With the advent of sound, particularly, and the emergence of the hypersentimental first Soviet sound film, Ekk's *Road to Life* (1931) as well as the Vasilievs' hyperpatriotic *Chapayev* (1934), it became clear that the potential for hortatory propaganda in the sound cinema was being encouraged; and indeed, the films of the thirties became even more heavily saturated with propaganda, while restrictions on artistic expression reduced the varieties of stylistic innovation possible.[46]

After the signing of the Nazi-Soviet non-aggression pact in 1939, all anti-fascist and anti-German films were withdrawn, including *Professor Mamlock*, *Soldiers of the Swamp*, *Alexander Nevsky*, and *The Oppenheim Family*. And while their withdrawal was justified as a measure necessitated by a change in the international political situation, it must be noted that several of these anti-Nazi films were also attacks against anti-Semitism, both at home and abroad. But it

[43] Utechin, *A Concise Encyclopaedia of Russia*, pp. 105–108.

[44] *Ibid.*

[45] David Rimberg, "The Motion Picture in the Soviet Union, 1918–1952: A Sociological Analysis" (Ph.D. dissertation, Columbia University, 1959), p. 77.

[46] *Ibid.*, pp. 77–78.

was in 1946, in the course of Zhdanov's campaign to "re-establish ideological conformity in the arts," that the Central Committee of the Communist Party issued a decree attacking a number of the then recent films, including Eisenstein's *Ivan the Terrible, Part 2*, Pudovkin's *Admiral Nakhimov*, and Kozintsev and Trauberg's *Simple People*. The general attacks against "foreign influences" in the arts had also, by this time, become inseparable from the virulent attacks of Stalinist anti-Semitism, which had been labeled "the struggle against cosmopolitanism." [47]

In 1938 all Yiddish language schools had been closed. Even as late as 1949 the harping upon "rootless cosmopolitanism," especially in the press, was a thinly veiled anti-Semitism which lingered; for example, it was during this period that a number of prominent Jewish writers and scholars were arrested and many subsequently liquidated. The Jewish Theater in Moscow and all but one Yiddish newspaper were shut down. And by 1952 the so-called Doctor's Plot against Stalin culminated in an outbreak of anti-Semitism so wanton that pogroms reappeared and rumors circulated about the possible deportation of all Jews to Siberian labor camps. (The Doctor's Plot involved an alleged conspiracy among several prominent Moscow doctors—most of them Jewish—to murder leading figures in the Soviet government, among them Zhdanov, whom the doctors were accused of having murdered in 1948. Following the death of Stalin in 1953, the plot was revealed to have been fabricated.)[48]

The cinema industry, with its high percentage of Jewish personnel, was especially vulnerable. On March 4, 1949, the Minister of Cinematography (then Bolshakov) launched an outright, personal attack on the director Leonid Trauberg in *Pravda*, accusing him as "the ringleader of the cosmopolitans of the cinema." [49]

The failing capacities of Soviet directors to maintain their traditional, uneasy compromise with the Party between cinematic experimentalism, propaganda, and entertainment value was exacer-

[47] Utechin, *A Concise Encyclopaedia of Russia*, p. 110.
[48] *Ibid.*, p. 24.
[49] *Ibid.*, p. 110.

bated by Stalin's now megalomaniac terror tactics and paranoiac attacks.[50] A low point in production, which had been reached once in 1933, was now being equalled in the years 1946–1952.[51] The Party openly directed filmmakers to understand that two themes in *all* films were now required as mandatory: (1) the Communist Party had to be depicted as the guiding force in all activities, and (2) Stalin had to be portrayed as personally involved in all decisions of any consequence.[52]

By 1946 the output of feature films had dropped to twenty, and by 1952, the year preceding Stalin's death, it reached the astonishing record low of five. (For comparison, one might consider that in 1951 India's annual production stood at 250, Japan's at 215, and the U.S.A.'s at 432.)[53]

Stalin's initial control of the film industry had been consolidated, as has been mentioned, as early as 1927–28, when he managed to eliminate most of his political opposition. Half of the 135 films produced in those two years, 1927–28, had been suppressed, thirteen being entirely banned, and over one-third, including Eisenstein's *October* (1927), restricted to limited audiences.[54] Now, in 1948, suspicions of Eisenstein's *Ivan the Terrible, Part 2* as a stylized, allegorical indictment of Stalin's autocratic despotism had arisen; and Stalin had it, too, banned for some eight years, until its release in 1958—five years after Stalin's own death and ten years after Eisenstein's—at which time Kozintsev and Trauberg's *Simple People* was also released, apparently with major cuts and revisions, followed by the eventual release of Lukov's almost forgotten *A Great Life* also in 1958, the attack against which had begun the postwar wave of repression.[55] A circle of constriction had been completed.

During the Stalinist years of repression, however, from 1927 until 1956 (when Khrushchev denounced Stalinism as the "cult of personal-

[50] Rimberg, "The Motion Picture in the Soviet Union," pp. 195–200.
[51] *Ibid.*, p. 200.
[52] *Ibid.*, p. 196.
[53] Utechin, *A Concise Encyclopaedia of Russia*, p. 111.
[54] *Ibid.*, p. 110.
[55] Leyda, *Kino*, pp. 390–393.

ity" in his "secret" speech before the Twentieth Party Congress), the most ironic circularity was the return in Soviet films to precisely those melodramatic, sentimental, and romantic excesses of traditional, pre-Revolutionary film narratives that the early experimentalists, such as Kuleshov, had polemically derided and so energetically striven to transform. Such films as Pudovkin's *Admiral Nakhimov*, Dovzhenko's *Michurin*, Vertov's *The Oath of Youth*, Kuleshov's *The Siberians*, and even Eisenstein's *Alexander Nevsky* and (although more contestably) *Ivan the Terrible, Parts 1 and 2* in part all belied reversions to a narcissistic dramaturgy—a cinematic self-portraiture of exceptional heroics and exemplary valor; gratuitous, predictable plots and characterizations; or a tired cinematography and montage in which the tried replaced the innovative—in fine, the very bourgeois attributes and stylistics that had so appropriately incensed the uncompromised filmmakers and theoreticians the Soviet experimentalists had once been.

ART OF THE CINEMA

ART OF THE CINEMA

Foreword

IN THE PAST we had no cinematography—now we do. The establishment of our cinema developed from Kuleshov.

Formal problems were unavoidable, and Kuleshov faced their solution. He was slandered because he was a pioneer, because all his energies were totally concerted in one clear direction, because he knew no other way.

Film work was conducted in an atmosphere of extreme vagueness. In order to break through the sticky and confusing tangle of seaweed, a sharpened razor's edge was needed. Henceforth, an ascetically rigorous direction came from the work of Kuleshov.

Kuleshov was the first filmmaker who began to talk about an alphabet, an organization of inarticulate material, and who worked with syllables, not words. This is what he stands accused of before the court of muddled thinkers.

Some of us who had worked in the Kuleshov group are regarded as having "outstripped" our teacher. It is a shallow observation. It was on his shoulders that we crossed through the sargassos into the open sea.

We make films—Kuleshov made cinematography.

—Pudovkin, Obolenski, Komarov, Fogel

Preface

"The Art of Cinema" is intended for:

1) Spectators
2) Executives of film studios
3) Filmmakers

To *spectators* because it is vital for them to know about the culture of cinema, about the methods and means of film structure. Having read the book, he will be better able to see films, better able to sense and appraise them.

To *executives* because "Administration disappears, art remains." Aside from the film apparatus, the studio, the laboratory, the business office, distribution, and money, the head of a film organization must be as well acquainted with film culture as is the viewer. A textbook familiarity is better than complete absence of experience.

To *filmmakers* because we must not build our work solely on individual experience and on "artistic inspiration." Tested methods, the experience of colleagues must be recognized and studied. I want to assist that process as much as I can.

—Lev Kuleshov

1: Montage as the Foundation of Cinematography

The purpose of my book is to familiarize the reader with my work—the work of the Kuleshov group.

I will not deal with the state of this method at present, but rather with how this method developed and what forms were found for it. The fact is that the work which my group and I carried out in cinematography began eleven or twelve years ago, and only in recent years, thanks to the revolution, thanks to changes in production organization, did it become possible for us to achieve meaningful results.

At first these were gained with great difficulty, and I consider it necessary to note those stages through which our work developed.

At the beginning of the First World War Russia's cinema was fairly large-scale; it had begun to produce merchandise, which went to the marketplace and returned a definite profit. Any number of people leapt into cinematography—actors, directors, scenarists, cameramen, all thirsty for easy earnings in a fresh field, but the film industry in Russia was so disorganized that some of questionable intent leapt into it. Thus, filmworkers consisted of a conglomerate of bandits, chiselers—people without any education whatsoever, who were eager to squeeze money out of cinema but who were uninterested in its cultural growth.

What is more, filmmakers became obsessed with writing about their work in newspapers and magazines. Some said it was a real art, others that it was not, that it was altogether nonsense, and so on.

Shallow articles and superficially enthusiastic reviews appeared. Even what seemed to be a critical controversy emerged, but it was not serious.

It was at this time that a group of people, interested as was I in serious cinematography, posed for itself a whole series of problems and took up their solution. Above all, we reminded ourselves that in order to determine just what cinematography was, it was necessary to find those specific characteristics and those specific means of impressing the viewer, which are present only in cinema and no other art.

Let us say if we are to examine any other form of art, such as music for example, that we should find a definite auditory content in it. Sounds abound in nature, and these sounds, this musical material, are fixed by composers into an ordered arrangement, placed into a prescribed relationship to each other (i.e., organized into a certain form) which is harmonic and rhythmic and thus emerge as a musical work.

Similarly it was quite clear to us what happens in painting: color too has a material form and it is this which is organized; so, in all other artistic crafts, it was equally possible to determine exactly the material of any given art, the means of its practice, and the method of its organization.

Yet when we began to analyze the filmic picture, it was very difficult for us to determine *what* emerged as its material, how this material was organized, what is the integral, basic impression-making means of cinema, what sets cinema apart from other forms of performance and from other arts. But it was quite clear to us that cinema has its own special means of influencing its viewers, since the effect of cinema on the viewer was radically unlike the effect of other entertainments and spectacles.

We then examined how a motion picture is constructed. In order to determine the main strength of the cinematographic effect, we took one strip of film, cut it apart into its separate shots and then discussed where the very "filmness" which is the essence of filmic construction lay.

Imagine that we have taken a passage of film in which superb actors played superb scenes in superb settings. The cameraman shot this scene very well. We projected this film onto a screen, and what did we see? We saw a living photograph of very good film actors, a living photograph of splendid sets, a well-filmed scene, a well-conceived plot, beautiful photography, and so on, but without cinema being in any one of these elements. It became perfectly apparent that cinematography is a specific thing, a photographic device that gives the illusion of movement, while what I was just describing has nothing in common either with the concept of cinematography or with the motion picture itself. In this example, we saw no specific methods of affecting the viewer cinematographically. Having arrived at these rather nebulous conclusions—that what we had viewed was not cinema, that it had no characteristic peculiar to it—we continued our research.

We went to various motion picture theaters and began to observe which films produced the greatest effect on the viewer and how these were made—in other words, which films and which techniques of filmmaking held the viewer, and how we could make him sense what we had conceived, what we wished to show, and how we intended to do this. At that time, it was wholly unimportant to us whether this effect was beneficial or even harmful to the viewer. It was only important for us to locate the source of cinematographic impressibility, and we knew if we did discover this means, that we should be able to direct it to produce whatever effect was needed.

We decided to begin our observations at the city's central cinemas, but it became apparent to us that for our purposes these were not the right places. First, a fairly wealthy public patronized these cinemas, and in a wealthy and well-educated audience it is considered in poor taste to display emotions: one must be reserved, and try to respond to what is taking place. Second, at that time people interested in romance frequented the more expensive theaters—where it was dark, where there were loges, and this whole setting was a convenient place to pass the time with a lady friend. And third, a rather large number of psychologically disturbed viewers went to the more expensive theaters, the "soul of Polonsky," the "soul of Maximov," "darling Kholodnaya—or Coralli," etc.*

The public in cheaper theaters, less educated, much rougher and more spontaneous, was not as neurotic and therefore reacted much more directly to the effect of the action and entertainment on the screen. Because of this, if that public was pleased by a particular scene in the picture, it applauded, shouting its approval; whereas if something in particular displeased it, it whistled and demonstrated its indignation unmistakably. It was easier for us to observe this public and to make our observations. Then it became apparent, first of all, that it was not Russian films but foreign ones that were the most popular.

It was foreign films that attracted the viewer most of all and forced him to react. This was easily understood. The point was that the technique of foreign films was finer than that of Russian films. The photography in foreign films was considerably clearer and sharper, the casting of actors more precise, the direction richer and more absorbing. Hence, in their clarity and in their technical aspects, foreign films attracted a larger audience than did Russian ones. Of foreign films it was the American ones that elicited the maximum

* These were the most popular screen stars of pre-Revolutionary Russia. R.L.

reaction, the greatest noise and applause. When it became apparent to us that American films were best in terms of their influence on the viewer, we took them for our study.

We began to analyze not only the separate shots of a film but studied its entire construction.

We took two films, for example—an American and a comparable Russian one—and we saw that the difference between them was enormous. It became apparent that the Russian film was constructed of several very lengthy shots photographed from a single position. The American film, on the other hand, at that time consisted of a large number of short shots filmed from various positions, because, it might be explained, for the price of admission the American viewer demands in return the maximum impressions, the maximum entertainment, and the maximum action. It was necessary in the American film to pack into the required number of reels the devil-only-knows how many incidents and to display them in the most interesting way since, I repeat, the American demands a full show for his dollar.

Thanks to this commercial determinant of the American film, thanks to the very tempo of American life, much more accelerated than the tempo of Russian or European life, thanks to all this, what caught our attention in the American film is that they consist of whole series of very short shots, of whole series of brief sequences joined in some predetermined order, as opposed to the Russian film, which at that time consisted of a few very long scenes, monotonously following one after another.

Working further, on comparing an American film to a Russian one in order to test its effect on the viewer, we became convinced that the fundamental source of the film's impact on the viewer—a source present only in cinema—was not simply to show the content of certain shots, but the organization of those shots among themselves, their combination and construction, that is, the interrelationship of shots, the replacement of one shot by another. This is the basic means that produces the impact of cinematography on the viewer.

The content of the shots in itself is not so important as is the joining of two shots of different content and the method of their connection and their alternation.

In American films, where shots very quickly alternate one with another, the combination of these changes is clearly perceived by the viewer. In a Russian film, shots changed very slowly, and the power of the effect which should come from these alternations was, in Russian films, incomparably weaker than in American ones.

Let us imagine, say, a fence ten miles in length. The first half is painted red, the second half green. The person who painted this wishes to elicit from a passerby a realization of the change of these two colors—the interrelationship of green and red—an understanding of how they vibrate together and are perceived.

Imagine too that for five miles you are walking beside the green color, at which point it changes and for five miles you walk along the red. Now imagine the fence is still longer—and another five miles is painted blue. By the time you reach the blue section, you will have forgotten that previously the fence was green, because you will have spent so much time perceiving one and the same color. If this fence were to change its color every yard—green, red, blue, red, blue, and so on, for fifteen miles—you would perceive a *combination* of these three color relationships all along the way.

The same happens also in cinema: during a long sequence, a lengthy alternation of scenes, you are not aware of the whole construction, the whole organization of the cinematographic material. During short sequences, during brief alternations, the relationships of separate sections, the general organization is made exceptionally clear for you. You immediately perceive it.

Thus, we came to realize that the source of filmic impact upon the viewer lies within the system of alternating shots, which comprise the motion picture.

The joining of shots into a predetermined order from which a film is made is technically called *montage.* Thus we announced in 1916 * that the fundamental source of cinematographic impact upon the

* Kuleshov's first theoretical essays appeared in *Vestnik Kinematografii.* R.L.

viewer, that is, the means on which it was necessary for us to work prior to anything else (leaving for a given period all other cinematographic elements, perhaps for several years ahead) is *montage,* that is, the alternation of shots.

Montage is the organization of cinematic material.

Hence, it became perfectly clear that separate shots, separately connected pieces of film, still did not constitute cinema, but only the material for cinema. We knew, of course, that for the preparation of this material it would be necessary to apply the strictest discipline and that extremely intense work would be needed in order that the quality of this material be of the highest order. But then we could not find time for this, since everything was so filled with theatricality, a false approach to cinematography, and such a total lack of understanding of the cinematic process, that temporarily it was necessary to set aside work on the actual material, to label it extraneous for the moment, and to direct all our attention and our labor toward the organization of material, toward the organization of the film, that is, toward *montage.*

For these reasons, we then proclaimed something that was not entirely accurate, namely, that it was not important *how* the shots were taken, but *how* these shots were assembled, how the motion picture was assembled. Let the material be wretched; the only importance was that it be well organized.

At the time that was a definite political step. Otherwise it would have proved impossible to bridge the gap in those minds upon which our work depended, because they were simply unable to grasp the grand scale at one swoop. We could not win on all fronts at once. The basic battle of our cinematographic faction, we announced, was the battle for *montage,* for the very *basis of cinematography,* and not for separate shots, nor for the material, which had to wait to be studied.

Fast montage was then called American montage; slow montage, Russian.

Moreover, by means of constructing their films according to the principle of rapid montage, the Americans produced effects never before seen by us. Let us visualize a scene: a person sitting at a desk, begins to think black thoughts, decides to shoot himself, takes a pistol from the desk drawer, puts it to his temple, presses the trigger, the pistol fires—the man falls.

In Russia the scene would be shot in the following way: the camera was set in place, facing the set, and it was reasoned thus: The man lives in a room, therefore it is necessary to build a room. We can't build four walls so—let's build three. In the room we must have windows and doors. The room must have wallpaper, flowered wallpaper, let's paper the walls. Paintings are hung on the walls. Flowers are placed on the windowsills. There must be a chest and a stove. We place all this in the room. The desk has writing implements, just as in reality.

An actor sits at the desk, imagines that he is feeling terribly despondent, takes a pistol from the desk drawer, brings it to his temple and fires. The cameraman films this entire scene, develops it, prints it, projects it onto the screen, and when the viewer looks at the screen, he simultaneously sees the curtain on the windows, the paintings on the wall, and so on. He sees a tiny actor among a large assortment of things, and while the actor is performing the juiciest psychological suffering, the viewer might be examining the leg of the writing table or the painting that is hung on the wall—that is, the spectator receives an extraordinarily distracted account of what is taking place on the screen.

The Americans filmed things completely differently. They divided each separate scene into montage sequences, into a series of shots that made up each sequence; in addition, they shot each separate moment in such a way that only its action was visible, only that which was categorically essential. Even in a long shot they constructed scenery so that details were not noticed. If they needed to achieve the impression of a room, they would achieve it by some simple detail. If the wallpaper design did not have a particular function, walls were darkened, or blackened, and only those objects were left in the light which were essential to the incident.

Besides that, everything was shot in what is called close-up, that is, when it was necessary to show the face of a person suffering, they showed only his face. If he opened the drawer of a desk and took a pistol from it, they showed the desk drawer and the hand taking the pistol. When it came to pressing the trigger, they filmed the finger pressing on the trigger, because other objects and the surroundings in which the actor worked, were irrelevant at that particular instant. This method of filming only that moment of movement essential to a given sequence and omitting the rest, was labeled by us the "American method," and it was thus placed in the foundations of the new cinematography which we were beginning to form.

Consequently, before beginning our experimental work and attaining any new results, we found our first working slogan contained in the following: "Separate shots of cinema film constitute cinematic material. Since we do not yet have the opportunity to work on the content of film material, we proclaim that for a period of time content will virtually cease to exist for us, and it will even be irrelevant for us. For the present we are working on a method of organizing the given material, that is, on montage, since montage is the main source of the power of cinematic effectiveness. That effect is evident only in cinematography and the optimum impression is attained only through the montage, when that montage is not merely of ordinary scenes, but of scenes filmed by the American method of shooting, that is, employing scenes in which every given sequence shows what is essential for the viewer to perceive, and shows them in the closest and clearest shots possible."

These were the basic conditions which we set forth prior to beginning our work. That was about ten or eleven years ago.

Now we are studying something entirely different in cinema. Yet, all that we are now concerned with grew from these basic premises.

The method that I am discussing yielded rather prodigious results: all that is well done in Soviet cinema is made by this method. All European and Soviet cinematography works according to this method but the Americans originated it. Now, having developed and used what was conceived by the Americans, we are carrying the work to a new frontier—the frontier of cinematic culture. But if the basis of cinema's effective influence had not been in our hands, then, of course, we would have never been able to achieve any results, for without mastering the material of film, we would have been unable to contribute anything.

Having established the work on montage as being foremost, we began to analyze montage itself and to establish its basic properties and methods.

What I am going to deal with now will, I think, appear simply amusing to everyone, it is so naive, so primitive, and so obvious. But at that time (and that time was rather recently) it seemed to be such incredible "futurism" that a bitter battle was waged against it. It was often necessary for our group, for my colleagues as well as myself, to discontinue our work because we were such formalistic revolutionaries. In my own case, it went so far that I had no money at home, no shoes to wear, and all because I was developing a particular cinematographic principle, which was simply "not acceptable."

The primary property of montage, which is now perfectly clear to everyone, but which had to be defended rabidly and with inordinate energy then, consists in the concept that montage creates the possibility of parallel and simultaneous actions, that is, action can be simultaneously taking place in America, Europe, and Russia, that three, four or five story lines can exist in parallel, and yet in the film they would be gathered together into one place. Ten years ago this elementary concept demanded an incredible struggle for it to be firmly established.

All the fundamental principles of montage, which I shall discuss, were first used by me in the film *Engineer Prite's Project* [1917–1918]. In shooting *Engineer Prite's Project* we encountered a certain difficulty. It was necessary for our leading characters, a father and his daughter, to walk across a meadow and look at a pole from which electric cables were strung. Due to technical circumstances, we were not able to shoot all this at the same location. We had to shoot the pole in one location and separately shoot the father and daughter in another place. We shot them looking upward, talking about the pole and walking on. We intercut the shot of the pole, taken elsewhere, into the walk across the meadow.

This was the most ordinary, the most childlike thing—something which is done now at every step.

It became apparent that through montage it was possible to create a new earthly terrain that did not exist anywhere, for these people did not walk there in reality, and in reality there was no pole there. But from the film it appeared that these people walked across a meadow and the pole appeared before their very eyes.

A few years later I made a more complex experiment: we shot a complete scene. Khokhlova and Obolensky acted in it. We filmed them in the following way: Khokhlova is walking along Petrov Street in Moscow near the 'Mostorg' store. Obolensky is walking along the embankment of the Moscow River—at a distance of about two miles away. They see each other, smile, and begin to walk toward one another. Their meeting is filmed at the Boulevard Prechistensk. This boulevard is in an entirely different section of the city. They clasp hands, with Gogol's monument as a background, and look—at the White House!—for at this point, we cut in a segment from an American film, *The White House in Washington.* In the next shot they are once again on the Boulevard Prechistensk. Deciding to go farther, they leave and climb up the enormous staircase of The Cathedral of Christ the Savior.* We film them, edit the film, and the result is that they are seen walking up the steps of the White House. For this we used no trick, no double exposure: the effect was achieved solely by the organization of the material through its cinematic treatment. This particular scene demonstrated the incredible potency of montage, which actually appeared so powerful that it was able to alter the very essence of the material. From this scene, we came to understand that the basic strength of cinema lies in montage, because with montage it becomes possible both to break down and to reconstruct, and ultimately to remake the material.

Now to proceed: After we shot this scene, at the time of editing,

* This was the greatest cathedral in Russia and once stood opposite the Moscow Art Museum and Lenin Library, but was demolished on Stalin's orders, to make space for a gigantic Palace of the Soviets, which however was never built. On the site now is a large open-air swimming pool. R.L.

we found we were missing one piece—we did not have the meeting between Khokhlova and Obolensky, who by that time were no longer available. So we then took Obolensky's and Khokhlova's overcoats—and, against the background of Gogol's Monument, shot two other people's hands being clasped in greeting. We intercut a shot of these hands and, because prior to this shot we had shown Obolensky and Khokhlova, the substitution remained absolutely unnoticeable.

This brought a second experiment to my mind. In the first one we had created an arbitrary earthly terrain; along a single line of movement we created an arbitrary scenic background. In the second experiment we let the background and the line of movement of the person remain the same, but we interchanged the people themselves. I shot a girl sitting before her mirror, painting her eyelashes and brows, putting on lipstick and slippers.

By montage alone we were able to depict the girl, just as in nature, but in actuality she did not exist, because we shot the lips of one woman, the legs of another, the back of a third, and the eyes of a fourth. We spliced the pieces together in a predetermined relationship and created a totally new person, still retaining the complete reality of the material. This particular example likewise demonstrated that the entire power of cinematic effect is in montage. With the material alone one can never achieve such unique, seemingly incredible things. This is impossible in any other spectacle excepting cinema, in addition to which none of this is achieved through tricks but solely by the organization of the material, solely by bringing the material together into this or that order. Let us take a simpler test: A person stands near a door. This is filmed in a long shot. Next, we go to a close-up, and in the close-up the head of another person is photographed. In this way, you can splice the face of Alexandra Khokhlova with the body of Nata Vachnadze, and again this will not be through trick photography but montage—that is, by the organization of the material, rather than by a technical gimmick.

After we had obtained such real achievements, after we felt a particular strength within ourselves, we established two other things. Before this, we had an argument about whether the particular psychological state an actor experiences is dependent or not on montage. There were those who said that here is something which could not be altered by montage. We had a dispute with a certain famous actor to whom we said: Imagine this scene: a man, sitting in jail for a long time, is starving because he is not given anything to eat; he is brought a plate of soup, is delighted by it, and gulps it down. Imagine another scene: a man in jail is given food, fed well, full to capacity, but he longs for his freedom, for the sight of birds, the sunlight, houses, clouds. A door is opened for him. He is led out onto the street, and he sees birds, clouds, the sun and houses and is extremely pleased by the sight. And so, we asked the actor: Will the face reacting to the soup and the face reacting to the sun appear the same on film or not? We were answered disdainfully: It is clear to anyone that the reaction to the soup and the reaction to freedom will be totally different.

Then we shot these two sequences, and regardless of how I transposed those shots and how they were examined, no one was able to perceive any difference in the face of this actor, in spite of the fact that his performance in each shot was absolutely different. With correct montage, even if one takes the performance of an actor directed at something quite different, it will still reach the viewer in the way intended by the editor, because the viewer himself will complete the sequence and see that which is suggested to him by montage.

I saw this scene, I think in a film by Razumny:* a priest's house, with a portrait of Nicholas II hanging on the wall; the village is taken by the Red Army, the frightened priest turns the portrait over, and on the reverse side of the portrait is the smiling face of Lenin. However, this is a familiar portrait, a portrait in which Lenin is *not* smiling. But that spot in the film was so funny, and it was so uproariously received by the public, that I, myself, scrutinizing the portrait several times, saw the portrait of Lenin as smiling! Especially intrigued by this, I obtained the portrait that was used and saw that the expression on the

* *Kombrig Ivanov*, 1923, shown in the U.S. as *The Beauty and the Bolshevik*. R.L.

face in the portrait was serious. The montage was so edited that we involuntarily imbued a serious face with a changed expression characteristic of that playful moment. In other words, the work of the actor was altered by means of montage. In this way, montage had a colossal influence on the effect of the material. It became apparent that it was possible to change the actor's work, his movements, his very behavior, in either one direction or another, through montage.

When we began making our own films, constructed on this principle of montage, we were set upon with cries of: "Have pity, you crazy futurists! You show films comprised of the tiniest segments. In the eyes of the viewer the result is utter chaos. Segments jump after each other so quickly that it is thoroughly impossible to understand the action!" We listened to this and began to think what method we could adopt to combine shots so as to avoid these abrupt shifts and flashes. Let us say that in a certain shot we have a moving train. Moreover, let us say it is swaying from right to left on the screen, while in the final frame of the previous shot the train occupied a position in the left-hand corner of the screen. However, in the first frame of the next sequence, the new subject took a prominent position in the right-hand corner of the screen. If you join these shots together, that visual leap from one side of the screen to the other will produce the sensation of an abrupt jump, will produce a nervous irritation which will disturb the viewer, not giving the impression of a smooth transition. Therefore, the direction of motion of the last frame of the preceding shot and of the first frame of the successive shot must coincide; if they do not, an abrupt jump necessarily takes place.

If one shoots a round object and intercuts it with a square one, then this should be borne in mind. If one shoots a close-up of a face but intercuts it with a face slightly smaller, watch out for these involuntary flashes and jumps.

2: The Material of Cinematography

Let us now consider an analysis of the cinema's material. We have quickly considered the time factor of the motion picture's construction; now let us move on to an analysis of its spatial factor.

If we were to consider a chair painted by an artist on canvas—what is more, painted by the finest artist, using the very best colors, on imported canvas, with every detail painted most realistically—if you were to look at this conception of a chair, you would be full of praise, because the chair would have come out beautifully, looking very real indeed. Now let us attempt to photograph this painted chair on film. Then, let us take a real chair, let us put it into an actual space, let us light it, and photograph it, too.

If we were to compare these two chairs projected onto the screen we would see that the actual chair, if photographed properly, would come out well. Then looking at the piece of film where the chair painted by the artist was photographed, we would see no chair there at all; we would see only the canvas, the texture of it, and the configuration of color in various combinations—that is, we would see only the materials with which the painted chair was made visible. It bears repeating that only real things emerge on the screen—that is, the interrelationship of various colors, the canvas, the flat surface—but the chair, as such, the chair drawn in three-dimensional space, the chair created by the artist on canvas, will not appear on the screen.

It becomes clear from this example that, before anything else, real things in real surroundings constitute cinematographic material; stylized material, the stylized representation of a chair will come out in cinema only as a stylization.

To proceed further, let us try to photograph human work—for instance, the work of an actor of the Kamerny Theater or the Meyerhold Theater, or the Moscow Art Theater. Let us try, on the same level, to film the work of a non-actor, or let us simply take a non-actor and have him play the same scene that the actor played. The scene consists of: a stevedore loading sacks of flour onto a ship. This is a labor process. Therefore, we will have sequences completely different in their human composition, albeit alike in their content, their labor.

When we view all these sequences on the screen, we shall see that the work of the Kamerny or the Meyerhold actor will not be communicated from the screen, because it will contain a whole series of affected movements, unnatural for cinematography, movements which by themselves emerge as stylized and do not produce that reality of content so essential in film. What the actor of the Kamerny Theater will do will not resemble the normal working process, will not resemble life, but will resemble only theater; the photography in the sequence will be a living representation of the theater with all its stylization and unsuitable elements for cinema.

Further, if we consider the work of the Moscow Art Theater actor, we will see that it fits the film much more, and that it emerges as much better, more expressive, more real. However, if we begin to analyze it piece by piece and observe everything that takes place in this sequence, we will see that, in the final count, the essence of the actor's work at the Kamerny and Moscow Art Theaters is the same; the latter's work has the maximum approximation to real living forms, while the former has the maximum distance from them, but neither is the material of reality needed in cinema.

If we simply choose a person, having no relationship to the theater, and make him do what we need, we shall see that his work on the screen appears better than the work of a theater actor and will give us more realistic material, from which subsequently it will be easier to construct a cinema film. If, finally, you photograph an organized process of work, this sequence—and only this sequence—will yield substantial cinematographic results. If you film a real stevedore, who is loading a bale, you will see that he strives to work in a way most advantageous to him, in order that in the shortest time with minimum effort he will complete his task. In the course of long years of work, he has developed certain habits of standardized, working gestures: he lifts the sacks deftly, drops them onto his shoulders, carries them well, simply and economically, unloads them, etc. This sort of work produces the clearest, most expressive, most efficient results on the screen. Of course, this sequence cannot be compared with the preceding ones, since all the preceding sequences will give a lesser effect: they are either saturated with theatrical stylization or are full of a poor relation to real objects, an inability to walk, to sit, to jump onto a streetcar, etc., etc.

Of course, if you need to shoot a footrace, an expert runner will appear best on the screen—a walking specialist, if you shoot a walking race. If we film some labor process, then only a very well-trained specialist in the given labor will produce the most expressive results.

Further, let us film, for instance, an autumn landscape: there is a ramshackle cabin, clouds in the sky, and a small stream nearby. Then you shoot a railroad bridge. Having examined both pieces of film on the screen, you will see that, in order to analyze your picturesque landscape, in order to perceive and analyze it, you need a great deal of footage, since everything in it is somewhat crooked, somewhat broken, and there are far too many different objects in it.

To understand the construction and basic lines of the railroad bridge, much less time is needed, because you are operating with very simple forms and directions which are quickly apprehended on the screen. If in order to show this sort of landscape and be sure that the viewer perceives it, let us say thirty feet are needed, then to show the bridge only ten feet would be needed.

Thus, from all these considerations, it is already possible to determine the basic line one must hold to in studying the material of cinema. The material of cinema must be extremely simple and organized. If a film is constructed by montage, then each piece will run for a certain short time. In order that everything filmed be seen, perceived, and understood in a brief given space of time, one must show the content of each piece in extremely concrete and highly organized ways.

Why, then, is the theater actor's work, which also is structured into given forms, unsuited for this? Because all the work of a theater actor is comprised of movements totally antithetical to those needed in cinematography. The point is that the audience in a theater sees the actor from various points of view: from the right side of the first row and from the left side of the gallery; one sits close to, another sits far from, the stage—and in order that the work of the theater actor may reach all the audience more or less in the same way, an actor develops a special style of gesture—the broad gesture. For instance, if it is necessary that an actor "bulge" his eyes, he does it in such a way that they may be seen from the very farthest point; if it is necessary to make some gesture with the hand, he does it in such a way that every member of the audience from both the right and the left, and from the center can see the given movement. During a long period of years theater culture was built upon this. It could not avoid taking into account the fact that the actor performed on a stage for an audience, which occupied an enormous area and comprised an enormous quantity of varying points of view, and for this huge space it was necessary to create one's work according to laws dictated by technical circumstances—the structure of the theater building itself. When the theater began to develop, no matter what style or direction it took, it was all the same: subconsciously this law, this rule of serving the needs of the audience, seated before the stage, always emerged and stamped its requirements onto all theatrical techniques. Regardless of the actor, regardless how closely his work approached reality (and the material of cinema must unconditionally be realistic: realistically existing and realistically arranged subjects), it is all the same: the laws of theater stamp their imprint on these techniques.

Cinematography, however, is constructed differently. With cinema every viewer sees the action only from one point of view—the point of view of the lens; he sees the action not from his own position, but from the position where he is placed by the filmmaker, shooting and editing the film. The filmmaker takes the viewer as if by the scruff of his neck and, let's say, thrusts him under a locomotive and forces him to see from that point of view: thrusts him into an airplane and forces him to see the landscape from the air, makes him whirl with the propeller and see the landscape through the whirling propeller. In this way, the viewer in the cinema is tossed about from place to place by the filmmaker and either approaches the subject, or finds himself in motion, or immobile, etc., etc. Consequently, the cinema viewer sees completely differently, on a totally different base, from the theater viewer. And regardless how cultured a given theater actor may be in his work, in cinema he is absolutely unsuitable inasmuch as his technique is founded on completely contrary principles, antithetical to cinema.

The conditions of shooting, from one point of view, present the opportunity for an exceptionally exact perception. Let us say, we have an angle made by a raised arm—then, the entire audience sees this angle of the raised arm as precisely the same, while in the theater this cannot be done, since there the action is seen in general and not from any particular point of view. Hence, the technique of the theater actor is totally antithetical to the technique of the film actor.

In the theater, in order to show a man shooting his antagonist and killing him, it is sufficient to produce a cardboard pistol, hit a drum once, for the person to start rocking, for the antagonist who is shot to fall—continuing to breathe—and the entire audience, even the most demanding audiences of the Moscow Art Theater, will be completely satisfied, it will seem to them that all this really happens this way. Therefore, in the theater in order to show one or another event it is enough to perform it, to represent it. In order to show the very same event on film, it is vital that the given event should realistically occur.

Here film technique comes to the rescue. Owing to technique, effects that seem unthinkable become possible. Let us take a fight, for instance. Of course, it would be best that the actors actually fight, that bruises appear, that they beat each other's faces and bodies with all their might. If you merely represent a fight, it will not work on the screen. It will appear as if a person pretends to stagger, pretends that he is in pain, pretends to be fighting. But thanks to film technique, you can produce a fight with utter reality on the screen, in addition to which it is not necessary that the actors really fight in order for you to film it. They can fight with the same degree of intensity and use the same direction of blows and movements as in an actual fight, but, by slowing down the shooting speed of your film, you can speed up the actors' movements and then it will appear on the screen that the actors are actually fighting, without in any way jeopardizing their physical well-being. Moreover, adding to the slowed speed of their performance the accelerated speed on the screen, you will have a realistic reproduction of the fight. To take another example, say we need to imagine a dead man, who is not breathing. We can always make a static frame, and the man will not be breathing. We can take a photograph, and then rephotograph it onto movie film. There is hardly a situation that cannot be made into an actual realistic event, and those situations certainly come out beautifully on film. But the moment you begin to imagine or suppose something, you immediately produce in film a theatrical fake. You get the very effect that you got from the painted chair. You will not have real meaning, real movement, you will have stylized movement, and stylization in cinema simply does not work—only real material by which film is expressed comes out.

This extraordinary love of cinema for real material explains what, in recent times, has been our attraction towards the newsreel. There are those who, quite independently of their original convictions, acknowledge nothing in cinema except the recording of actual events in the newsreel.*

Why is this so?

Because the newsreel uses a maximum of real material and everything appears absolutely real and authentic. But even in the newsreel, if you show chaotic, disorganized movement with uncertain directions and aims, the viewer must expend enormous energy in order to sort out the chaos taking place within the rectangle of the screen. In order that the viewer may clearly and easily read from the screen what he is expected to, movement is needed, movement with direction on the screen in an organized, rather than in a chaotic, form; in addition to which the material must not only be real, but organized within a given rectangle, on a given plane, which in cinema is constant.

In cinematography we always have a plane with its sides in a definite relationship and for this plane, for this rectangle, it is very easy to discover its own laws. If one does bring out these laws and

* A probable "dig" at Dziga Vertov with whom a methodological rivalry was developing. R.L.

follow them, then no matter what takes place on the screen, it will be extremely easy for the viewer to comprehend what he watches.

Imagine for yourself that we have a rectangular screen, and on this plane some primitive motion is taking place. If this movement takes place parallel to the top and bottom of the screen, the position of the given movement in relation to all borders of the screen and in relation to the given plane is perfectly clear for the viewer to apprehend. If the line of movement abruptly inclines at an angle of forty-five degrees, you will apprehend it very easily and clearly, and its incline and direction will be clear to you. If the incline were to vary, however slightly, you will perceive these small inclinations and changes in relation to the given rectangle only with the greatest effort.

Therefore, if you construct a certain movement upon the screen along a straight line parallel to the top and bottom and along a straight line parallel to the right and left sides, that is, perpendicular to the previous one, joining all the little quadrates, then all the directions will be extremely clear and plain to you and a very small amount of film will be needed for them. If crooked lines are introduced into this given grid, on the basis of the given movement, the crooked lines will likewise be easy to apprehend. The more complicated the construction of the grid, however, the more it will confuse—the greater will be the energy and time expended on that which is shown on the screen. That is why a railroad bridge or a cityscape, constructed on clearly delineated patterns, is read more clearly and distinctly than a landscape with clouds, trees, water, grass, houses, etc., because the lines of a house are somewhat crooked, a cloud is neither round nor square, the form of this landscape is so indefinite that one has to spend a great deal of time in order to read the screen clearly and distinctly. In the final analysis, you will not come away with the same impression from this landscape as you would, for instance, from the view of a bullet fired from a pistol. The shot should act as a sign, as a letter of the alphabet, so that you can instantly read it, and so that for the viewer what is expressed in the given shot will be utterly clear. If the viewer begins to get confused, then the shot does not fulfill its function—the function of a sign or letter. I repeat, each separate shot must act as each letter in a word—but a complex type of letter, say, a Chinese ideogram. The shot is a complete conception, and it must be read instantly.

In order to present to the viewer a given shot, as a symbol, one must give it a great deal of organizational attention, and for this there are very limited means. In cinema you have a given plane—the four-sided screen, which has no depth of light stereoscopically. Therefore, in order to give maximum expressiveness to the symbol, one must exploit the given plane of the screen with optimal economy—in other words, there must not be one piece of superfluous space on the screen, and if you show something which cannot occupy the whole surface, then all excess must be eliminated. The screen must be filled to the maximum and totally used. It must not have a single millimeter of unused space. Every tiny piece, every quadrate on the screen must not only be put to work, but put to organized work in simple, clear, expressive forms.

These considerations have led to the establishment of the technical training of film actors. I shall describe this technique and this school later, but now I shall briefly digress, for otherwise what is to follow may not be clear. Let us deal with the following: We have established that real material must be operative in cinematography. Imitating, pretending, playing are unprofitable, since this comes out very poorly on the screen. If a person is snub-nosed and you make him a longer nose with putty, the counterfeit will be detectable in a close-up and the nose will not seem real but will look stuck on. If you need a tall, stout man, but your actor is thin, and you pad the thin actor with cushions, and the like, the result on the screen will be a perfectly formless, cotton-wool scarecrow, the movements of which will never correspond to the basic construction of his figure. In other words, the result on the screen will be obviously false, theatrical, a prop, a game.

Arising from these circumstances, we issued a timely announcement that: owing to the technique of film actors being quite distinct from that of theater actors, and because film needs real material and not a pretense of reality—owing to this, it is not theater actors but "types" who should act in film—that is, people who, in themselves, as they were born, present some kind of interest for cinematic treatment. That is, a person with an exterior of character, with a definite, brightly expressive appearance could be such a cinematic "type." A person with an ordinary, normal exterior, however good-looking he may be, is not needed in cinema.

In film everything is constructed on established interrelationships, of people with varied characters. In order that a film actor justify what he does, he must have an appearance that corresponds. No good actor can be made to remold himself, to make himself over into another type, since in film no make-up, no costuming will work. No short man can be made tall, no thin man made fat. Therefore, it is quite clear that a motion picture must be made from the start with that group of chosen people who represent in themselves interesting material for cinematic treatment.

If a given tall man can so contract his muscles that he can transform himself into a short man, that is the epitome of remolding. If a person with high eyebrows can in a given moment lower his brows, he is thoroughly suited for film. The model can transform himself as many times as he pleases, but only insofar as all this is accomplished on the basis of real material. Insofar as this is done externally by means of putty, by artificial thickenings and changings rather than physical ones, it is inapplicable to film. Here I state reservations: It is, of course, possible to paint a woman's lips, to paste a beard on a man almost unnoticeably because the art of make-up is now sufficiently developed. Yet, experience has shown that if one films an actor with a fake beard, it will appear much worse than a real beard.

If one really attempts to adapt the actor's art to the screen then one must approximate, as much as possible, newsreel material and provide actual, real material. Further, if we have people to write film scripts and scenarios, then the entire work of the scenarist and director, since they determine the character of a given work, must be based on real material. If in a group we have a tall, thin person, this in itself could determine a whole series of film stories, but if, say, the story demands a third person, whom we don't have or who isn't specially trained, the result will be so weak that it is useless to invent situations for nonexistent material. Every piece should be constructed on suitable material. For example, if you shoot a film in Batum based on a story of the North Pole, it will not work. What pertains to nature, pertains also to people.

These types who are to work in acted feature films cannot simply perform the jobs as posed by the scenario. They must play their roles in the finest, most organized method. Everything they do, all their working processes, must be precise, clear, and plain, convincing and optimally organized, because otherwise they cannot be well apprehended on the screen.

I shall give another example, which I have frequently observed in the film school. When a person waiting to prepare himself to be a film type comes in and he is told that the room is hot—open a window—he begins to imagine heat, approaches an imaginary window, acts as if he is opening the window, and so on, he is unable to perform a simple, real task—to take hold of a real window and open it—what is more, to do this with maximum ease, maximum simplicity, as any other task, which should be done in the most efficient possible way. Occasionally, to this type of work is added a characteristic mannerism which defines a given type, but even this is done by physical means and not by acting—for example, by movement along crooked rather than straight lines, movement along angular lines or flowing ones; but the actual plan of the disposition of a given work must still come in an organized form.

Now I return to what I began with. All these considerations gave birth to our school for the cinematographic training of people. Before anything else, in order to teach a film type to move in an organized manner, to control his own physical organism, and ultimately to fulfill any given task—in order to take into account the entire mechanism of work, the entire mechanics of movement—we divided the person into his component parts. The point is that the quantity of human movements is as limitless as the quantity of sounds in nature. In order to play any musical composition, it is enough to have a definite organized range—a system of sounds, upon which an entire musical system can be based. In the same way we can create some sort of system of human movements, on which any movement proposed can then be based.

We divided man into basic articulations (movements).

We examined the movement of limbs as movements along three axes, along three basic directions, as, for instance, the head as the articulation of the neck.

A movement along the first axis was the movement of the head to the right, to the left. This gesture corresponds to negation. A movement along the second axis—up and down—is a gesture corresponding to assent. A movement along the third axis was a tilting of the head toward the shoulder.

The eyes have one axis along which they move to the left or right and another for upward and downward movements; unfortunately they do not have a third axis, and the rotation of the eyes around is a combination of the first and second axes.

The collar bone (clavicle) has the movement of the shoulder as its first axis forward and backward, on its second axis no mobility, while on the third, it can move up and down.

The shoulder and the entire arm from the shoulder move along the first axis forward and backward, on the second axis upward and downward, and on the third axis have the movement of "twisting" and "turning."

Then come the other bodily parts: the elbow, the hand, the fingers; then the waist and the leg—the hip, knee, and foot. If a person is to move on all these fundamental axes of his bodily parts and their combinations, his movements can be recorded, and if his movements clearly express these combinations of axial movements, they can be easily comprehended on the screen, and a person working can take into account his work at all times and will know what he is doing.

As an actor considers his work in relation to his environment, so must that environment be correspondingly taken into account. The environment in which an actor works is a pyramid, the top of which converges to the center of the lens. This space—which is taken by the lens at angles of 45° – 50° – 100° and which must be fitted onto a rectangular screen—can be divided into those basic quadrangles which provide an outline for movement with such precision that they occupy a very clear and easily decipherable position in terms of the rectangular screen.

If a person works along clearly expressed axes of his mechanism, and movement along these axes is distributed within the space allocated on the screen—in the "spatial grid"—you will get the maximum clarity, maximum purity in the work of the actor. You will read everything he does on the screen as clearly as in a mirror.

If a whole series of labor processes need to be performed, each of those actions must be optimally organized, and it is very simple to organize them—thanks to the presence of the grid and also thanks to the presence of axes in the human mechanism. In order for a person to learn how to operate, without thinking about it, along his axes and by a given grid, there is a special set of exercises, a special kind of training, which brings one into a condition similar to that given in the training to drive an automobile. The whole secret to driving a car lies in its being driven automatically; that is, one does not consciously think about when it is necessary to shift gears, as all of this is done mechanically and instinctively. It is a poor driver who thinks about when it is necessary to accelerate and to shift gears; and a good driver who, when he is asked how often he changes gears, can never answer the question, because he performs it all mechanically. The qualified film actor, whose entire technique is calculated to give an efficient reading of his screen performance, is the result of precisely this same sort of training.

Working along these axes, it is vital to remember that the entire film effect is a series of labor processes. The whole secret of the scenario is contained in the author's giving a series of labor processes; to wit, even the act of pouring tea or kissing is a labor process, in that in both of these acts there is a known set of mechanics.

I must repeat: Only organized work comes out well in cinema.

I must repeat: A "type" who cannot alter his appearance by the manipulation of his muscles is not sufficiently cinematically trained; such a "type" is not suitable for work in film.

3: Concerning Scenery

I began my work in cinema as a designer of scenery. I worked with Evgeny Bauer on the film *Thérèse Racquine.* After I was given preliminary instructions, I made the sketches and brought them to the studio. In them all the ornamentation, the shop windows, signboards, and other details of the arcade—the main setting of the film—were painstakingly designed and colored. Everything I showed them was accepted as "nice pictures," but at the same time I was upbraided in the most merciless fashion. It became clear that the building of film decor was not dependent on whether a wall is to be painted in this or that fashion but in the very construction of the decor itself, that is, in the form in which the decor is laid out, in what is the relationship of the walls to each other. What is important is the plan of the room, its construction, and not the finish, not the external appearance. The greater the variety of corners, passages, staircases, the more variations, even in an ordinary living room, the more interesting this is for the camera, because corners, passages, stairwells, staircases, landings, provide opportunities to use cinema lighting to the maximum, and to structure the acting in the most interesting, expressive fashion. The work of the set designer should not consist in giving his designs the overall appearance of decorations but rather in the drafting, construction, and measurement of the plan of an arena for cinematic action.

Generally, when artists came to the cinema, they approached the construction of set decorations purely as painting, whereas at that very time the foremost set designers were constructing their decorations more as architecture rather than painting, and a very important method of set decoration for the film was developed by them in the use of the foreground close-up, consisting in the fact that the character of the set, its significance, its sense, is expressed in the foreground close-up, located in front of the camera itself.

Some sort of large-scale object would be placed in the foreground —either a column, or an arch, or some sort of other characteristic object; in addition to which the object was so chosen that it embodied the properties and peculiarities of the entire set. It became clear that detail in the foreground greatly heightened perspective, gave the photography greater plasticity and the perception of the decoration greater relief, and to the extent that cinematography tends to lessen depth and stereoscopic effect, this characteristic device became most useful. I was particularly absorbed with the use of this method at that time. I was always thinking of how to find an especially novel foreground piece, so as to make an especially characteristic and interesting set. A special term was born in the studio: everything that was conceived for the foreground was described as a "curiosity."

The next stage in the work on set decoration was the utilization of already existing decorative material. To construct always newer and newer decorations, new furniture, new ornamentation, is very expensive, and in the last analysis it does not produce such great artistic results, while the material outlay does not justify itself either artistically or commercially. It became necessary to think in terms of utilizing those elements of decor already in our own studio or on the lot where sets are constructed. I had just then designed a railroad station set, which had been constructed in the following manner: on one side was the glass partition of the studio, very closely resembling the glass partition of a railroad platform where trains arrive, and on the other side was a wall constructed of wooden boards, placed rough-side out. These planks, placed rough-side out and reinforced with wooden beams, were covered with grey paint, giving the impression of a concrete wall, reinforced by iron girders.

Yegorov, the designer for the film *At Sea* (1916),* built the decor of a ship. He made it very simple: erected funnels, then an exhaust pipe for a ship's ventilator, made a ship's railing for the deck, cleared the entire studio, and put an ordinary basin filled with water at its end. The entire set stood against a background of black velvet and was lit so that a beam of light fell onto the basin with the water, producing light reflections on the water: the water shimmered, glittering in ripples. The foreground—the funnel, the ventilator, and

* This film was based on a Chekhov story of the same name; the film's release title was more salable, *For the Right of the First Night.* R.L.

the railing—was similarly lighted, and everything else was darkened. On the screen it gave the full effect of action on a ship at sea: the water in the basin under the expertly placed light gave a total impression, the full illusion of a seascape.

After my first experiences in the construction of sets, I came to study the director's work. I concerned myself first of all with experiments in montage and the acting of non-actors.

Thus, work on set decoration was deferred. I only came to grips with it again when, in actual practice, I began to apply my directorial experience to the production of films using rapid montage. To the extent that it was necessary in these films to learn from the Americans, since the entire culture of montage derived from American cinematography, it became necessary to study American scenic design, to familiarize oneself with its characteristic properties, its peculiarities.

From this moment, a new period in the work on set decor begins: the planning of perspective is simplified, and material and the quality of material move into first place—that is, one does not simply take walls covered with this or that kind of decorated wallpaper, but already utilizes the *material of the walls;* in other words, the first thing to be considered is *what* these walls are *made of.*

Our tests began with a maximum use of planking. It became necessary to build sheds or interiors in such a way that the walls and flats would not be covered with wallpaper, but with a facing of boards, in addition to which, if a poor or simple room was required, the boards were fitted one to the other and never separate; if a luxurious room was required, then the boards were planed, painted, covered with lacquer or shellac, and sometimes enclosed in separate frames. Sometimes, instead of planks, white sheets of veneer were fastened into the frames, which also gave the appearance of an even, smooth wooden surface of expressive material.

In *The Extraordinary Adventures of Mr. West* [1924], a great number of reversed planks were used, since they already had the appearance of veneer, enclosed in frames and slats. These sheets of veneer produced very expressive, clear and eye-pleasing material. A still greater factor dictated the use of wooden set decoration, namely that the planking in our factories was in an abysmal condition (this was at a time when the ruined Soviet cinema had only begun reconstruction): planks were warped and crooked and when wallpaper was pasted on them they gave the impression of crooked, cracked walls, no matter how they were lit. Yet when wooden sets were made from either boards or veneer or reversed planks, their appearance under any lighting was completely satisfactory.

All these constructions, however, were made by us according to a complex plan, that is, with a large number of corners, passages, and breaches. This was done by the cameraman, firstly, in order to provide great space for the utilization of light and shadow; secondly—detective themes of the films of that time also required as many breaches in the set as possible—either so that it would be possible to conceal oneself, steal up, or jump out of hiding, or so that there would be obstacles that would have to be surmounted, so that there would be material for a fight, pursuit, and so on. Later, when it became necessary to depart from the primitivism of American detective thrillers, when American montage was already mastered, when the elementary technique of the non-actor was charted, we passed on to more complex problems in montage, theme, and acting. This transition immediately altered or, more precisely, sharpened our attitude to set design. It became clear to us that the less that set decor is noticeable, the less attention the viewer pays to it, the less it interferes with the *action* of people, objects, etc., the more it will serve as a background assisting the action—the better the decor will be. We wanted the action, that is, the main element in cinema film, to be most lucid, in relief, and the background to be shaded, to serve only a subsidiary role.

Human physiognomy, objects, and all kinds of action emerge best on a darkened background; objects appear most sharply in relief on black velvet: they can then be lit best, they can then be best seen. Thus, it became perfectly clear to us that if we could make a darkened or partially darkened decor, then this would present the most suitable background for movement and action.

It is not necessary to invent anything extraordinary for this, because in the finest examples of world cinema, a darkened decor has often been used. In several foreign films we saw the merest suggestion of decor, just enough to imagine the setting in which the action is taking place.

When close-ups are shot, however, when the non-actors or required objects are to be located near the decor, then one must achieve the maximum expression of the qualities of the material from which the decor is made, and the better the surface finish of the decor, the better the result: it becomes more realistic, more genuine.

Thus, the final stage of work on set decor is that the decor is constructed with the calculation that it can be darkened, that it will serve as a dark background for the action, reckoning with the maximum expression of the qualities of its material.

Walls are covered with plaster or a special putty. Smooth, rough, regularly rough, and roughly coarse surfaces are all used. The same applies with regard to wood: it had been used previously, except that prior use of wood surfaces appeared to be insufficiently worked out. The fact is that earlier, in order to bring out the design of the grain of a wooden surface, a primer covering was attempted. But a primer coat gives the wood a semi-shiny gloss: hot spots appear on the screen, "halos" which are too white, too contrasting; while the structure itself—the grain of the wood—becomes indistinguishable.

Then came the attempt to cover the wood with oil-based paint. If one or another grain-pattern was needed to simulate, let us say, oak or redwood or karelian birch, it had to be artificially surface-grained with mat oil-based paint, that is, in the same way that office doors are covered. Moreover, glossy oil paint is not suitable any more than primer paint, because it produces very severe highlights and halos. It is vital to mix oil paint with beeswax—then it produces a mat reflection and appears even-looking on the screen.

Concurrent with this, the exploitation of material for wall covering was begun, because wallpaper, as has been earlier noted, almost always produces negative results due to the warpage of the planks. Velvet turned out to be the most suitable, and, it is said, the Americans cover even the exteriors on their sets with velvet! All these blocks and arches of the buildings, the foundation stones of huge structures, are covered with velvet. It has an ordinary grey color, produces an even surface on which light is evenly distributed. The walls of interiors covered with velvet or broadcloth of various colors likewise produce a quiet photographic tone, which appears well on the screen. Any set decor, no matter how well constructed, is lost in poor lighting. Therefore, the latest system of working with set decorations has become such that the background of the set decor need not be lit.

Decor and its background ought to be as simple as possible in construction and as darkened as possible. Only that action is lit and made manifest which takes place against the background of the decor, primarily by back lighting. Sets are generally built in such a way that at the top of the walls, opposite the camera, lights are positioned which *illuminate* the action taking place against the background. General diffuse lighting is thrown from the front and the side, in addition to which masking screens are placed next to the light source—the spot or flood—which mask the light from falling onto the walls of the set. But the bright light for effect, the spotlight producing a sculptural effect of the figure or the object being shot, that light is placed behind, that is, it projects from the tops of the walls in the direction of the camera.

Such filming of the set produces the most expressive result, and the majority of standard shots ought to be made in this manner.

If one must work with brightly lit backdrops, in order to show the set decor itself as primary, then it is necessary to use screens of velvet or broadcloth, because that material will provide the means to distribute the light on the walls in the softest, most diffused manner.

On the basis of the conditions effected, it was possible to prepare the decor of the *The Female Journalist* [1927, also known as *Your Acquaintance*] with some precision. Rodchenko, who designed *The Female Journalist* for me, grasped my requests very quickly and produced sets which the cameraman, Kuznetsov, was able to light in such a novel way that they interfered neither with people nor objects nor the central action, but facilitated and simplified their perception. The sets for *The Female Journalist*, in the main, were painted either dark brown or totally black; some were made bright red. They were lit so that the presence of the walls could be felt—even the design on the wallpaper; but at the same time the decor was darkened as much as was necessary, so that a human face or an object would stand out against the background brightly and in relief.

Ordinarily, when a painter is invited to work in the cinema, he feels it his obligation to demonstrate his extraordinary zeal in decorative sensitivity. He wracks his brain in order to think up a clever set design that is effectively decorated and is so often disappointed when the director or cameraman spends little time filming his decorative product. If one were to shoot the set decor of a painter in the way he would like, then one would get a film not about the action nor the subject of a picture, but a film about the contrivances and inventions of the set designer, and the entire attention of the spectator would be drawn to it from the start. Thus the decor must be shot so as to function as a montage sign, as a piece of the plot, as a scenario detail—then, of course, one must display the decor in full. When the decor serves little particular importance, except as characteristic of a certain place of action, then it ought to be shown within the action in the sparsest and most unobtrusive manner possible.

The most necessary economy in the setting of objects and details was applied for the first time in *The Female Journalist*. Generally, in the past, if one had to depict a given room, everything in that room which would be there in reality would be hung on the walls, placed on tables, in cupboards, etc., and when the viewer saw this overcrowding, he would not be able to make out either the actors or the objects in the shot, and would confuse it all, mix everything up with everything else. In order to perceive all this, more time is needed than a given piece can continue according to the requirements of montage. Every piece of action has its limited length: in montage construction it has its beginning, it has its end; it is extremely clear in the limitation of its length. And all this overcrowding of unnecessary, mundane things does not lend any character to the decor whatsoever: it produces the most horrible hodgepodge, confuses everything, and the result is, of course, lamentable.

It appeared that even today, just as twelve years ago, at the very beginning of my work, one had to find a "curiosity," one needed to emphasize in two to three details the basic character of the given structure.

Only those objects are needed in the decor which are necessary for the action. Everything that stands simply because it is customary for it to stand in a given instance, or everything that hangs because it is customary for it to hang in a given situation, is entirely superfluous, is easily removed, giving an opportunity for the viewer to perceive the shot better.

If, for example, the decor requires a writing desk, it is customary to place on it candlesticks and photographs and a paperweight and statuettes, scattered papers, etc. Such a writing desk comes out looking very bad; a host of unnecessary things confuses the perception of the viewer and forces him to tire himself needlessly.

If one must come up with some knick-knacks, some absurd objects, in order to depict who the owner of a given desk is—some sort of absurd person who has to do with absurd objects—then it is not necessary to pile a whole heap of these things: for this, one characteristic object that expresses everything at once is sufficient.

Rodchenko has described in his article on the work on *The Female Journalist* an example of such use of an object. When we needed to construct the room of an actress, from whom the journalist was buying something, whatever we tried, whatever tasteless objects we dragged in, nothing worked out. When we carried everything away, removed everything, leaving only—on a wall shelf—a ridiculous looking glass elephant, while by the divan we put a coat hanger in a vase, it was sufficient to reveal the entire essence of the room. And everything else only confused and concealed the characteristic properties of this room.

In the work of Rodchenko for *The Female Journalist*, I consider especially successful the chairs in the conference room of the Iron

Combine, already familiar from accounts in the press. These chairs turned out particularly expressive, because they were extremely well situated in the given decorative space. That same metrical spatial grid of which we spoke when we were analyzing cinematographic material and the construction of the shot, applies equally to the mounting of the settings; chairs placed according to the basis of its laws, produced the best shots of the film. Only the clear interrelationship of objects is well and easily comprehended on the screen. The simpler the placing of objects in the shot, the clearer the placing of walls and platforms, the more expressive and understandable the result.

One of the most painful questions of set construction for Soviet film studios—painful because our studios are still so impoverished—is the question of the construction of floors. Floors in studios are usually of boards, and, what is more, of the sorts of boards that are only suitable for the representation of a woodshed or very poor rooms. In ordinary rooms, a parquet or a plain smooth floor is needed most often. The simplest solution is to cover the floors with carpets, except that since carpets come with designs, it is best of all to lay them not face up, but face down—wrong side up. The wrong side does not have a design and comes in a rough mesh, dark grey in color, appearing very smooth.

To secure a good parquet or an even, plain floor was always exceedingly difficult. Until the present time, we did this in the following manner: we took a thin sheet of veneer and painted the parquet pattern on it in oil paint. The pieces of veneer were assembled, then covered with lacquer, and a shiny parquet floor resulted. Generally, the joints, the fittings of these veneer sheets are splintered, disfigured, and the parquet quickly stains, quickly becomes dirty and loses its design, such that it becomes totally unnoticeable, while the luster, which results from the lacquer, gives off an unacceptable halo and harsh white spots when photographed, and the result is—no result from a floor like that.

Until the present time not one Soviet film studio has laid real parquet or parquet made from sheets of thick veneer. If parquet were made from twelve millimeter veneer, and covered with designs and not lacquered, but waxed, that is, if real parquet were produced, then it would be unconditionally photogenic. It seems that only in Pudovkin's *The End of St. Petersburg* [1927] has this experiment been performed and has given good results.

Earlier, when I began to work in the cinema, a fairly effective floor was made at the Yermoliev studio: it was covered with shiny oil-cloth, but, due to the unevenness of the studio floor and the weakness of the oil-cloth, this method did not prove itself.

The most amazing floor that I have seen in the cinema was made for *Rosita* [1923, U.S.]. This floor, completely glass-like, reflected figures on its surface. How it was made we don't know. According to all appearances, this was either a glass floor, or a very fine parquet covered with liquid glass.*

Completing the analysis of set decorations, I pass on to the camera operator, with whom the work of the set designer must be joined. Not knowing the basic rules of the camera technique, not knowing in its entirety the utilization of sunlight and artificial light, the set designer will never produce satisfactory construction for motion pictures.

4: The Work of the Cameraman

When experimental works of cinema with unexpected camera angles began to appear and were regarded as new, we left-wing filmmakers declared we saw no inventiveness there.

Constructing our cinematography based on American examples, the most perfect examples of cinema culture extant in the world at that time, we got examples of "new" angles, "new" set-ups for filming from our teachers. Shooting from waist-high cameras proved impracticable much earlier, and our teachers were already applying new methods, new camera angles, with success.

The fact is that the nature of cinematography itself dictated the

* The designer of *Rosita* was Sven Gade, brought from Germany by Ernst Lubitsch for his first American film, made for Mary Pickford. R.L.

birth of new methods for determining the shot. And the necessary conditions of the film—the presence of montage—necessitated that the shots be constructed simply, clearly, distinctly. Otherwise, the "flickering" of a rapid montage would not be sufficient for a full scrutiny of its contents.

We noticed that the most distinct, convincing shots were those of technological and architectural content. Railroad bridges, skyscrapers, steamships, airplanes, automobiles, etc., by appearing best of all, created the film aesthetic of that time. Animals, organized processes of human labor, children, appear just as convincingly and clearly—as opposed to actors and acting, painted landscapes and such beauty and art. The reason our first classic films showed a preference for historical rather than countryside scenes is that the latter came out so badly. Later, when technological material became boring, when the Americans glutted their own market with it, a reaction set in: film distribution overflowed with rural and domestic subjects. The following appeared: *Tol'able David* [1921], *The Old Homestead* [1922], and the famous *The Covered Wagon* [1923].* These films were very good ones, good because by then the technique of shooting had become exceptionally perfected.

From its first utterance, cinematography required a wealth of technical material. In this way, the fashion for new settings, for photographs and the material for photographs, came somewhat late for us filmmakers. Moreover, we knew that these innovations appeared in our films due to the nature of cinematography, due to its unique and technical properties. The "aesthetics of constructivism" did not enthrall us in any way. Life showed that, despite the colossal service of the affirmation of new photography by the transfer to it of the principles of cinematography, innovators were caught in the impasse of filming houses from above and below.

This happened because new still-photographic shooting techniques did not evolve *organically,* while new cinema shooting did evolve *organically,* having come from the nature of film and film stories.

* *Tol'able David* was directed by Henry King from a Hergesheimer story; the last two films were directed by James Cruze and photographed by Karl Brown. R.L.

The basic difference between cinema and theater can be seen in the different perception of the spectacle by the viewer. In the theater, action is observed from various, but for each viewer fixed, points of view. Everyone sits in his own seat, and everyone sees the spectacle taking place on stage from his own point of view. In the cinema, even though the spectator is sitting in his seat, immobile, the camera is moving and shifting for him: the film spectacle is taking place before him not from his, the viewer's point of view, but from the point of view of the moving camera.

The montage of the film provides the opportunity to show action not only from the outside, but from the point of view of the characters themselves.

The hero looks away and sees something. If the hero is on top of a staircase, or a tower, he sees the action from the top down, and conversely, those who look at him from the ground see the action from the ground up. An object or a face can be shown "small-scale" (long-shot), and in the event of its necessary distinctness, can be shown "large-scale" (close-up) across the entire screen.

A fight is ensuing; one of the people acting is being flipped over in the heat of the fight—a new point of view: a whirling set decoration, in the eyes of the man being whirled about.

Thus techniques of shooting from new points of view were born.

Further, action taking place before the camera must be shot in such a way that it can be easily perceived.

The shot should not strain the attention by being overcrowded and likewise should not contain unused empty spaces. For example, our cameramen seem unable to compose a close-up of a human face. In ninety-nine out of a hundred cases, they shoot so that there is an empty space above the head, which is completely unnecessary, weakening the full strength of the shot.

Now imagine for yourself that a crowd scene is being shot: a group of people are talking amongst themselves, more people approach them, a crowd forms. The crowd disperses, a man walks through an opening in the crowd. If we shoot this whole scene from the usual point of view, from waist high, then we would barely see on the screen the scene I describe. This would happen because the human figures would conceal each other; the plan of action, its spatial formulation, would not reach the viewer, because it would not be shot by the camera. In a large part of the scene the actors would inevitably mask each other, screen each other. Therefore, very often the most efficient shooting of any action is from a high angle, but only in those cases when it is essential (as has been already shown). Apart from that, high-angle shooting strengthens perspective, which is very valuable for the cinema, since the motion picture camera gives little stereoscopic effect.

The film shot is not a still photograph. The shot is a sign, a letter for montage. Any change from a normal point of view ought to be used by the director with an awareness of the work of the shot as a *sign.* A proud person may be shot from a low angle—the foreshortening will stress, will help to highlight the emphasis on pride. An oppressed or dispirited person may be shot from a high angle—the dispiritedness will be emphasized by the point of view of the camera. Example: the work of Pudovkin in *Mother* [1926].

Superfluous things and superfluous space must be eliminated from the shot. The proportions of the screen do not always permit the showing of necessary action in such a way that it would be placed on the screen without superfluous surroundings.* For this the Americans employed the iris. This is an expanding and contracting circular diaphragm that is placed before the lens of the motion picture camera, with the result on the screen of a black background with a light circle of action in the middle. The dark edges of the diaphragm are in shade and reduced to nought. (There is another inner diaphragm, built in between the two elements of the camera lens. It serves to control depth of focus and alters the aperture of the lens.)

By means of the iris a particular compactness of the shot may be achieved. Anything superfluous in the shot is removed. Those who consider shooting with the iris for mere beautification and aestheti-

* A problem discussed by Eisenstein in 1931 in "The Dynamic Square"; see his *Film Essays* (Dennis Dobson: London, 1968), pp. 48–65. R.L.

cism are deeply mistaken. This diaphragm has a great working significance, and it does not provide a beautiful frame nor should it provide one. Of course, if it is incorrectly used, the result is negative. Everything must be properly used—this is beyond doubt. I cite examples of incorrect use of the iris:

1. When the iris is too sharp. It should not be used on light backgrounds; it is best in shots with a dark setting or a dark background.

2. Under no circumstances should a mask instead of an iris be used to limit the frame—that is, a metal plate with various cut-outs placed in front of the lens, resulting in a vignette effect due to its sharp edges.

3. It is bad if the iris is used not for limitation of the frame or the elimination of what is unnecessary, but to make the shot pretty.

A mask is used for showing action seen through a keyhole, through binoculars, etc.—then its cut-out shape has a function.

The iris is also used for showing action taking place in the distance, in memory, and for showing "what is to be seen" as distinct from "who is seeing." In such a case, it becomes a conventional designation, to which all have become accustomed and as it were, have agreed to understand in these ways.

As can be seen from what has been said, the point of view of the shots and the differing nature of what is photographed depends not on trying to be original nor on the mere desire for novelty no matter what, but on the organic and technical problems of cinematography.

The cameraman and the director must work along new lines, but always reasoning and justifying what they do, otherwise the result is mere aestheticism and a senseless distortion of the shot.

Somewhere in the thickets of our film-world, in the "depths of time," were born the prejudices and "classic rules" for the cameraman. From teacher to student, from comrade to comrade, absurd practices and traditions are passed on. How difficult it is for a cameraman—even the most qualified—to discard groundless habits overnight.

A theory exists, for example, that in a long-shot of a landscape the horizon line must separate the top third of the frame from the bottom. Aren't there enough examples of superbly expressive shots taken with the horizon not along the top third?

Comrade Kuznetsov, who worked with me on two films so marvelously, don't you recall how we argued at the start of our work about the horizon line? And later did you not yourself select those shots in *By the Law* [1926] with the horizon falling along the bottom tenth of the frame, and even shots that were completely without horizon?

Now that you are one of the finest Soviet cameramen, hasn't it become easier to work, after you and I buried that good old tradition which was worth about a cent?

Let art photographers work according to canons—we shall construct our shots by logic and economy. In the past, a man viewed everything from eye level, from a moving horse, at best from atop a hill. Now, he can observe and perceive from everywhere, and what is more, with variations of speed. Cinematography will assist him in this. The viewpoints of a coalminer or a deep-sea diver are as accessible to the screen as the viewpoint of an airplane pilot.

Now let us pass on to another, most important element in the work of the cameraman—light. The ability to utilize, to organize light is central to the work of the cameraman. The most advanced, the best leftist photographers and cameramen do not possess the rudimentary skill of using lighting, and lighting is the essence of photography and film photography.

To obtain satisfactory shots, it is necessary that the subject photographed be lit. Elementary: there is the subject, the light is in front of it—which means it can be shot. That is the way shots were made in the beginning—with head-on illumination by sunlight. What happens on the screen? Objects do not have a clearly expressed form and merge with the surrounding background. Imagine that a cylinder or a column is being shot. The column would be flattened, in the same tonality as the things near it and behind it. Flat lighting is often used in the cinema, and therefore the photography looks blind; everything runs together, somehow everything seems cut out of paper.

Objects lit from the side appear best on the screen.

Imagine, again, a cylinder or a column: the shape of the column, its cylindricality, will stand out sharply and clearly with the use of side-lighting.

But in shooting several objects, in a filled frame, shot with side-lighting on the shadowy side of the objects, the result is again monotonous, flat, and grey. Side-lighting reveals and accentuates the minutest details to be found on the object.

For the short pieces of the finally edited film, it is necessary to generalize the elements in each shot. The simpler and more economically objects are arranged and the clearer plastically they are in themselves, the better the shot communicates from the screen.

Therefore, the most advantageous lighting for the cinema is backlighting, so-called *contre-jour.* This light provides the opportunity to see, precisely and clearly, the silhouette of the object, provides an effect of stereoscopy and depth.

Imagine a high-voltage electric station. Its construction, the openwork of its buttresses, will be shown best with backlighting.

Doubtless a combination of back- and side-lighting would give the maximum expression of what is being shot; with that kind of lighting we can get a maximum result on the screen. It is imperative to note that working with such combined lighting or only with *contre-jour* is technically the most difficult.

I shall explain why. The motion picture camera is not yet perfect. If we shoot two objects simultaneously, one, which is very light, say, satin-stitched embroidery on white material, the second, which is very dark, say, satin-stitched embroidery on brown material, what we shall get on the screen will be either well-exposed black embroidery, with all the light gradations, or a light-flared white one. To get a good definition of both simultaneously is exceptionally difficult. To do this one must use special accessories, light filters, etc. Moreover, a pleasing result is not always attained. To attain satisfactory, normal photography it is necessary to *manipulate* the highlights, the half-tones, and the shadows to get a good definition. Utilization of these three elements will produce a comprehensible, sharply-defined picture on the screen.

Repeatedly, in practice, either light or shadow is overexposed, deprived of intermediate tones.

In shooting scenes of nature with backlighting it is usually very difficult not to overexpose the shaded side. Harsh backlighting then produces only silhouettes, edged with a halo, seductively appealing in its prettiness but not producing a clear, simple photograph. For the backlighting that we are discussing must be functional, and not an affected "aesthetic." In order to shoot with backlighting, it is necessary in most cases to use artificial light and to make use of sunlight reflectors or mirrors, or floodlights and electric lamps.

That is why in shooting newsreels it is especially difficult to achieve high-class photographic results. The imperfection of our film technique makes it impossible to shoot whole series of very important events in life around us. When the very highly photosensitive film is widely distributed, and when it will become possible to achieve the same precise exposure and definition of light and shadow, black and white, the material of cinematography will be extremely enriched. It will be self-evident that, using backlighting, we achieve the optimal functional effect: a fusion of the positive qualities of side- and backlighting.

One should not think, however, that one can shoot only in this way; one can also shoot with flat lighting, but only when necessary. Everything that is written in this book is written as the result of a certain degree of experience in film work, but the findings established are applicable only in a *majority* of cases; exceptions are not only possible, but are necessary, as long as they do not destroy the fundamental, primary propositions.

Exceptions, as just mentioned, might be shots that are of intentionally high contrast: thieves carrying a flashlight, creeping across a room, or a face lighted by firelight from a stove, etc. Front lighting produces extraordinarily effective results with the use of light filters. Example: a bright, white-hot, sunlit rye field against a background of black sky.

Hardly any of our photographers or cameramen, even the very famous ones, know how light functions and are able to use it spontaneously.

Usually, during the action, the background has a secondary significance, often serving as an indication as to where the action is taking place. The components and details of the background are often superfluous, with the exception of those cases in which the furnishings, the surroundings, play a secondary role.

Direct your attention to the thoroughness with which the experienced Americans treat this, even in their ordinary films. Recently, I saw two inexpensive American pictures. In all the exteriors, as well as interior shots, the director so arranged the action that shots were always made against a dark background. Either the entire scene was lit while the backdrop was shaded or while, with a lighted backdrop, the actors passed in front of a dark doorway or dark drapery or a shaded area of the background.

Now let us move on to the work on decorations and to the work in the studios.

Let us enumerate the basic tasks of the director and the cameraman we have indicated:

1. The selection of the point of view for shooting.
2. The clean, simple composition of the frame—clear and distinct use of light.
3. Calculation of the degree of exposure for highlights, half-tones, and shadows.

All this pertains equally to shooting in sets at the studio.

How do cameramen ordinarily do their shooting in the studio? The set, let us say, is a room. The action takes place within it. As in exteriors, the simplest thing is to use front lighting, so it is simplest to "light up" the entire set. If one had but to set a single front light source, this would be only half the problem. It becomes necessary to set many light sources, because for sufficient exposure, the intensity of each studio lamp by itself would be insufficient. For the average set, ten to thirty various lights are set up (floods, spots, projectors, arcs).

One essential property of the motion picture camera should be noted: the more one closes down the lens aperture (an inner diaphragm between the lenses), the sharper the focus, the clearer the image on the screen. But the smaller the diaphragm opening, the less the illumination through the lens, and accordingly, the more the set must be lit. Fearing unsharp shots, cameramen generally set up an extraordinary number of lamps on the set. What happens on the screen?

The lighting is both from the front and from different angles. What results is an irritating fragmentation of light. People and objects cast a large number of half-noticed shadows on the background, light beams transect each other. As a result the lighting hodgepodge utterly ruins the work of the director, the actors, and the set designer. Both in real exteriors and interiors there are limited light sources. In nature, the sun and the moon cast light, sometimes bright, sometimes diffuse, dimmed reflections and refractions of the light from highlighted surfaces. In the daytime the light in a room comes from the windows, partially through doorways, bright or dimmed, and is reflected, bounced off highlighted surfaces. In the evening there is the light from lamps, of which there are not really that many. Therefore, the need to light the set from multiple points of view, just so it should be bright, is absurd. The flat distribution of the light—we know from analogous examples in exterior shooting—exacerbates the feebleness of a given shot. Accordingly, the work of a cameraman in the studio must come down to the fact that, for shooting, the minimum number of lamps be set up. In addition to which, the intensity, the amperes of each separate lamp must be increased to the maximum. It is imperative to work on the problem of "overheating." With overheating, with easily overloaded lamps, the amount of ultraviolet rays from the voltage arc, which the camera records, is increased. Diffused background lighting, in which the set is bathed in light, is produced by lamps that will spread it most softly; the ideal for basic diffused lighting is the mercury lamp. The plan of lighting apparatus on a studio stage should be as follows: for half-tone exposure, everything to be shot is lit with diffused lighting, which is completely flat, not intense, and coming from banks of lamps.

Clarity of action should be achieved with a minimum number of high-intensity lamps, since they fulfill the basic work in the production of the cameraman. As with exterior shooting, the principle of backlighting with supplementary lights is the best, so intense light, principally directed from the back and side, must be utilized, while the general "background" of light fulfills the role of supplementary lighting.

In the chapter on set decoration, I fully detailed the basic methods of lighting sets. When *The Extraordinary Adventures of Mr. West in the Land of the Bolsheviks* [1924] was being shot, our film industry had only just emerged from its crib. In the newly organized Goskino Film Studios, *Mr. West* was the second picture to be shot. Not only was there no suitable lighting apparatus in the studio, but even the central heating did not work well. With what enthusiasm, with what frenzied energy we worked then, and how this enthusiasm and energy, then and later, was knocked down by the bureaucratism and mediocrity of the "fake" studio executives! Our lighting was principally with Kliegs and "arcs," lamps with one pair of carbon terminals, built mainly by the lighting designer Kuznetsov (the cameraman's brother). Background lighting came from antediluvian "Jupiters" (a type of carbon filament arc lamp)—lamps with dual focal points, thoroughly unsuited for the job. And what startling results in filming were achieved by Alexander Levitsky, the first Soviet master cameraman, and assisting him, the light designer, V. Kuznetsov! For the first time in our cinematography, Levitsky applied an extraordinarily simple economic design of light. There were very few lighting units, and there was nowhere to obtain new ones. The proper loading of the lamps gave the necessary intensity. Kliegs and "arcs" successfully took the place of "spots." It is true that the actors suffered from constant burns and stood the risk of sustaining heavy injuries from the constantly falling carbon. It was not feasible to put up protective netting, since it would have shielded the light. Eyes were scorched among most of those shot in close-ups. Constant delays and breakdowns of the lighting, carbon burns, scorched eyes, demanded an incredible application of effort. I feel obliged in these reminiscences to note the extraordinary discipline and the virtual heroism of the workers in my collective. During the shooting of a close-up, Komarov did not move from the spot when a dilapidated, very heavy door fell onto his head. Sletov, while smashing a pane of glass with his bare hand, sustained deep cuts but categorically insisted on continuing to work. Khokhlova, contracting measles at the studio, went on shooting with a temperature in excess of 104°F. Galadzhev, out on the street and nearly naked, rubbed snow on himself in freezing weather. In his pajamas, Podobed was filmed in the frost, and so on. And all this was the result of the desire to give a good start and a boost to cinematography in our studios. In an interview with a reporter, I described the faulty lighting projectors and the falling red-hot carbon (the temperature of the crater of the carbon arc is 3600° Celcius), and when this was published, the head of Goskino gave me the harshest reprimand for not keeping secret the technical squalor in the studios.

Now we work with more or less perfected German lighting equipment. But still, instead of simple, sharp, clear lighting, most cameramen produce an unbearable variegation of light and overexposed shots. What would have happened with those shots of *Mr. West*, which demonstrated, first and foremost, that we were far from helpless, if they had been shot by a different cameraman?

The cameraman and the entire film crew must be possessed of a particular ability to adapt to conditions. The shortcomings of technical equipment and poor shooting conditions ought to be used for a film comedy.

But from this it should not be inferred that studios need not build, order, supplement their technical equipment inventory with the latest improvements.

Above all, film workers should remember that our nation and our cinema are still in an extremely precarious material position. We must adapt and innovate as cleverly as possible, in order to attain maximum results. Generally for work on our scale, the most incredible items are demanded. Very recently, I conducted a most complex shooting assignment in Moscow with a talented but inexperienced cameraman. What he ordered to be sent out to him for some night shooting! Needless to say, despite all efforts, it was not possible to get everything. With colossal difficulty I convinced him to shoot with what was available. I suggested a whole host of lighting tricks to overcome the shortcomings. For instance, campfire smoke was used and it was easy to light it, since the play of the smoke produced the effect that made up for the shortcomings of the lighting. Long-shots had to be taken with only what was most essential being lit, only in the center. All around, everything remained in darkness, and, of course, the result was thoroughly satisfactory. Necessity forced us to complete the exterior shooting quickly; it was impossible to wait for light, sunny days. The weather was grey, foggy; the sun was barely shining. Yet, shot through the fog, the sun produced extraordinary results. This experience again demonstrated how much better it is to apply oneself, to make use of existing conditions, and not to wait, not to demand, without fail, one's accustomed shooting conditions.

One must experiment, attempt to find in unfavorable conditions the unexpected photographic effect.

Osip Brik once told me: while standing in his comfortable spot, a cameraman shooting the newsreel of a funeral, shouted to the procession, "Coffin toward the camera!"

I worked with Khanzhankov as a set designer and built sets, which were to be shot by a very fine cameraman. Having left the studio for a while to have breakfast, I was interrupted by the cameraman's shouts. It seems that the set did not fit into the frame, and he was demanding that the set be moved farther from the camera.

Poor soul . . . he did not realize that it was possible to move the camera backward—there was plenty of room.

In our time—in dreaming of work in American conditions—we jokingly said we would sneak into the storeroom and slightly spoil the film, or else we would not be able to contend with ideal conditions, and the results must be poor!

In the beginning, our *montage* theory of film editing was opposed also because of the difficulty of working with new methods.

Editors would have to splice the most minute pieces, actors would have to train more thoroughly, cameramen would continually have to change their set-ups, to climb, clamber quickly and reorient themselves, and move again. But in the past it was free and easy! A cameraman shoots a take of 300 feet, cranks the camera handle, alternately with his right then his left hand, so as not to tire himself; and at the 150 foot mark announces laconically: "You forgot to remove the ladder."

I think the best job of shooting in our studio recently was accomplished by Konstantin Kuznetsov in *The Female Journalist.*

The fundamental principle, mentioned in Chapter 3, "Concerning Scenery," is as follows:

A set tends to be particularly dark. Lamps which can be directed toward the necessary action, are placed on the top of its walls for the purpose of back- and side-lighting. Diffused lighting provides the fundamental exposure, the walls being almost completely shielded from the source of illumination.

It should not be forgotten that in film everything indispensable must be clearly and precisely visible.

The use of light for beautification, darkening what is necessary, making shots flashy, back lit *contre-jour* à la Rembrandt, is absurd, trite, and useless.

I categorically warn against this hazard.

The shot must be, above all, light, clear, and comprehensible. Any superfluity whatever should be removed or darkened.

A preoccupation with effect may produce an unjustifiable, muddled "Rembrandtism."

Work more simply! Don't be pretentious or sophisticated; build your fundamental construction more solidly!

5: On Scenarios

Pure action constitutes the basis of the film scenario. Movement, dynamics—these are the material of the film-spectacle.

That is the reason why people, starting to work in film, when they familiarize themselves with it properly, invariably experience a passion for silent film without subtitles.

The origin of this fascination is obvious: dynamics, pure movement always nourish the cinema film; conversation and, consequently, subtitles, seem foreign, unnatural elements of the scenario.

Though it is wholly comprehensible, this tendency is not correct. Of course, a subtitle, like the transmission of dialogue, like the transmission of anything that does not constitute film material, is unnatural in the silent motion picture.

The shortcomings of film art must not be replaced by surrogates—subtitles. A good subtitle must function just like a shot. A subtitle is the same sort of film material as the exposed pieces of the film, lying before the director on the editing table.

Generally, a film is cut and then subtitles are added—this is incorrect. Subtitles and shots should be edited simultaneously.

Of course it is often necessary to repair a film, to correct, to alter it by subtitles, but repair is another matter; good merchandise should not require repair.

I have already said that it is necessary to think in shots, that is, in conceptions of the to-be-photographed objects and actions, edited and arranged in a story.

If one has an idea-phrase, a fragment of the story, a link in the entire dramatic chain, then this idea is expressed, laid out in shot-signs, like bricks.

A poet places one word after another, in a definite rhythm, as one brick after another. Cemented by him, the word-images produce a complex conception as a result.

So it is that shots, like conventionalized meanings, like the ideograms in Chinese writing, produce images and concepts. The *montage* of shots is the construction of whole phrases. Content is derived from shots. It is better still if the scenarist gives the content by determining the character of the shot-material. The director expresses the conception of the scenarist by *montage* of shot-signs.

Let us suppose that a scenarist or a director evolves the concept of a certain episode. He should not conceive the content of the episode first and then search out visual material for its formation. The concept of an episode, and one's reasoning about it, should arise from visual images, from that material which will be filmed. Moreover, different cuts, a different construction—the montage of shots—can change the concept of an entire episode. Windows opening, people looking out, galloping cavalry, signals, running boys, water gushing through a break in a dam—these can be edited, say, either as a festival, or as the construction of a hydroelectric plant, or as the activities of hostile forces in a peaceful city (my example is borrowed, I think, from Pudovkin).

In order to think in scenario terms about the "triumphant explosion of a dam" or the "charging of hostile forces into a city," what is needed is not a literary method, but a filmic one—in shots: galloping horses, marching infantry, explosions, and so on, imagining them as if on the screen, visually.

With this method of work, naturally, the thing conceived will be filmic, and easily given form by the director.

Let us trace the evolutionary forms of the scenario, examining its different aspects. We turn again to the Americans, who are so strong in standardized merchandise. Their average films are made by all the proper filmic rules. As it begins, the standard American film—during the first third—is a bit tedious, static, slow in unfolding.

The second third is filled with an intensification of dynamic or psychological action. Here lies the center of the conflict, the unfolding of the plot, etc.

The final parts are filled with maximum film dynamics.

The most simple movement—running, wrestling, a chase, struggling with the greatest number of obstacles and in furious tempo—cut in quick montage, forces the viewer to concentrate the remainder of his attention. Moreover, this is called forth by an intensification of the film material, pure action, primarily by fighting or competition.

The American construction of the film is very logical; the viewer will always watch something thus constructed, because his attention is naturally distributed.

The first steps in pure filmic work on a scenario, naturally, come down to a saturation of the film with a maximum amount of action. This gave birth to detective stories with their chases, fights, pursuits, etc.

The overproduction of detective thrillers and adventure films indicated to directors and scenarists other subjects—of a domestic or psychological character. To give high quality film form to such themes appeared extremely difficult. The inner dynamic—the situation of a person in his ordinary life with a minimum quantity of elementary filmic movement does not fit well into film action, which above all requires pure movement. The fundamental error in the work on psychological subjects was this: that various states of being of the characters were revealed only through the expressions on their faces.

When something unpleasant happened to a hero or heroine, the whole sense of the cinematic depiction came down to the most absolute demonstration in mimicry of unpleasantness on the actor's face. As a result, an unbearable, false, and artificial genre was created—a psychologism inadmissible in the cinema, particularly theatrical and unreal.

Yet in such themes there were pieces filled with a hidden dynamic, a possible origin of elementary filmic action.

It seems to me that the director, Anoschenko, produced successful examples of this.

People calmly sit on barrels of gunpowder and wait. And only the viewer knows that the barrels are about to explode.

In a scene like this, people display no emotion and act minimally—they sit normally, but the tension in the viewer's apprehension of the episode undoubtedly exists.

A preoccupation with psychologism, quite useless for the cinema, approached such extremes that one director asserted: Cinema is not when the hero loses at cards, but when, standing by a window, he looks at the street and thinks about having lost.

Two international masters created a school of cinematography; these two masters are D. W. Griffith and Charles Chaplin.

Griffith either works with pure film dynamics or on the pure emotion of his actors, making them portray their psychological states by means of complex movements of their whole bodies.

But these movements were not elementary grimaces, but were reflexological, very precisely worked out, which is why they achieved their aim. With Griffith, actors did not merely bulge their eyes, say, in terror, but created other movements, which communicated their states of being more truthfully.

Lip biting, fidgeting, wringing of hands, touching of objects, etc., are the characteristic signs of Griffithian acting. It is not difficult to surmise that they are approaching moments of extreme emotion and even hysteria.

The whole of a film cannot be built entirely of powerful emotions, which is why Griffith fills the intervals between emotional climaxes in his scenarios with pure film dynamics.

Constructing his films in this way, he has achieved extraordinary results, and his work and scenarios were unsurpassed for a long time.

But it was Chaplin who transformed the classical scenario in *A Woman of Paris* (1923). In its construction, this scenario can be considered as ideal in its display of new methods of film work. Chaplin virtually reduced to nought the elementary ways of showing emotions in the face. He demonstrated the behavior of a person through various events in his life by means of his relationship to things, to objects. The way in which the hero relates to his environment and to the people around him changes because of his state of being, and alters his behavior.

Thus, the whole task is brought down to the establishment of certain labor processes, because something is done with objects, either disrupting or restoring their normal order; in dealing with them either rationally or senselessly, the actor demonstrates labor processes. A labor process is nearly mechanical; therefore, movement; therefore, the absolute material of cinematography. Thus, the work of the scenarist must come down to the development of a plot through the relationship of actors performing with objects, through man's behavior and his reflexes. *A Woman of Paris* showed that these are undoubtedly filmic and can be more interesting than just elementary movements.

Many say that *A Woman of Paris* turned out well not because the scenario was good: "We would never have accepted that scenario for production!" An absurd explanation; it is precisely because of the scenario that *A Woman of Paris* is exceptionally good.

Everything in it proceeds from one thing to the next in an unbroken logical sequence: not one episode can be discarded—or the unbroken cinema-dramatic chain will be lost.

When our people attempt to emulate the Chaplinesque scenario, they string out, one after the other, a senseless series of episodes of a person with objects so that each one can be discarded or changed. The scenario of *A Woman of Paris* is extraordinary because nothing can be discarded, every episode in it is necessary and obligatory. If the scenario of *A Woman of Paris* were given to a poor director, the film would unquestionably turn out well, but with Chaplin, it became a work of genius.

Our cinema has always suffered from the poor performances of actors and the poor composition of the shot; that is why the virtuosity of Griffith's work was unattainable to us for a long time. At first, the fundamentals of Griffith's method were analyzed at the State School of Cinematography, later G.T.K., and our films—it is true, not for the most part and only recently—showed genuine film techniques.

Yet, Chaplin's scenario method yielded almost no results, because in its application what we discussed above was not taken into consideration: the necessity of acting through reflexes, through the behavior of a person, tied to a firm logical linkage of scenario details. Our *Women of Paris* were a conglomeration of more or less lucky tricks of individuals and objects, lacking a fundamental, logical line of a film story.

And utterly unable to work in new ways, technically perfected directors and actors made provincial, senseless imitations of such things, leading to the most pitiful results.

The following types of scenarios exist for us:

1. The scenarios that take as their material the simplest filmic action. Their success depends on properly thought-out stories. Generally, things are made with an average degree of compositional quality but achieve success due to new and correct themes.

Examples: *Red Imps* (1923), *Strike* (1924), *Battleship Potemkin* (1925).

In these films the diverting quality of movement, the conflict and resolution based on new Soviet material, achieved great popularity for them (*Red Imps*). The historical events of the revolutionary struggle cannot but seize the viewer, as in *Strike* and *Potemkin*, shown in a series of cleverly conceived episodes, for they did not actually use a new perfected film technique, but only utilized new Soviet themes, under cover of which only occasionally does a new cinematic form show through. That is why the success of such scenarios is so frequently a matter of chance. Their quality is in the material of the episode, and not its cinematographic treatment. That is why after the cinematic recognition of *Potemkin* came the artistic failure of *October* (1927) and after the amazing success of *Red Imps* came the oblivion of Peristiani.

2. The second fundamental type of scenario—that which utilizes the results of previous film culture, constructed with a recognition of its principles, experience, and methods, and developed in terms of our Soviet themes.

Examples: *Mother, The End of St. Petersburg.* These, while they have several shortcomings, mainly of a directorial character and not due to their scenarios, are nonetheless in the main genuinely cinematic, not fortuitous—films of quality, culture, and conscientiousness in their production.

3. The third type of our scenarios is a conglomeration of the most diverse subjects, either imitations of foreign subjects; or domestic and national subjects, with a generous use of accordions, Leghinka dances, operatic trappings, and costumes; or "suspense" dramas; or detective thrillers; or pseudo-industrial films . . . and on the whole—failures.

Why? Because in these scenarios there is insufficient material for the depiction of the behavior of a person through his relationship to his environment. If there is, then it is only as a collection of invented stage-business with objects, lacking logical filmic connection and the inevitability of its existence, and in the worst instance not even elementary filmic action.

4. The fourth type of our scenarios is a scenario of an experimental, innovatory character. In these scenarios, successful or unsuccessful attempts are made to establish the study of new film forms, new expressive means in cinematography.

Both the FEX group and a whole host of young maestros create such works, most coming from left-wing artistic groupings or from film schools.

It is not necessary to discuss their significance—it is obvious: without such work there will be no genuine film culture.

Resting on one's laurels and the absence of investigation into form will inevitably lead to catastrophe.

The biggest, most important error of our scenarists consists in the fact that they write scenarios not derived from existing material but rather from "within oneself"—they simply fantasize. That is why our films:

1. are inordinately expensive;
2. always inaccurately portray new modes of life;
3. never achieve characterization through type-actors;
4. are shot half-heartedly by directors.

To be sure, the administrators of our film studios and the scenario-literary-artistic departments are more at fault in this than our scenario writers. Only through the study and use of the materials of everyday life with actable roles and of a technically filmable nature, etc., is it possible to create genuine film works.

If the organization has the opportunity to use an airplane, a train, and, let us say, the North Pole, then it is essential to construct the scenario on these bases.

If, however, an airplane, a train, and the North Pole appear in a scenario and they are difficult for the organization to obtain, then the cost of the film soars beyond reach.

If a scenario concerning everyday life is created, it is essential that the scenario be born of the phenomena of everyday life, that it be evolved only from these, it not being possible in any other environment, in any other conditions of life.

Otherwise, a film-opera will be produced, and an opera is not filmic material—this is obvious to everyone now.*

I repeat, in everyday life material the story is born from the circumstances of the given environment and not simply attached to it.

We have not been able to make full film use even of factories.

Every film director wishes to be ideological, and each of them zealously appends to a romantic drama this or that sort of factory production.

Change the factory, let us say, from a glass factory to a cannery, it is all the same—love remains unchanged. Why, then, based on which indications is this or that production selected? Is it really so difficult to understand that drawing room dramas take place in the drawing room, and that the same situations cannot be altered by costumes and factory backgrounds? The product itself ought to dictate the subject. However, we are often carried away by such films.

Either Averchenko or Teffi† tells the story of a young authoress who had written a play and showed it to the director of a theater. He demanded that the authoress turn the drama into a farce. The authoress changed nothing, only before each character's name she wrote "naked," so that it would be risqué as in farce.

So it is with our ideological scenarios: the characters in them are workers or communist party members, and the setting is a factory, only not organically but by the old recipe—naked!

Chaplin attained such extraordinary results from the work of the actors in *A Woman of Paris* principally because he was shooting it for nearly two years. In producing the film he was simultaneously training his actors.

* True, I recall that a fine opera director named Lapitsky headed the production department of Kino-Moskva, and that a contract was signed with a superb operetta artist named Yaron, but the film value derived from this was minimal.

† Two popular writers of feuilletons. "Teffi" (or Taffy) was Nadezhda Buchinskaya. R.L.

While such a method of work is possible for American cinema, we cannot spend so much time in the production of one film. How, then, to achieve ideal work with actors?

Actors must be educated and trained in advance; each studio must have its own qualified cadres. Each director must have his own group of workers, trained, with complete mastery of film technique.

Scenarios should be especially written for these people; then the quality of the actors' work will be guaranteed. If one has to search people out and train them according to the scenario during the shooting, there will be neither sufficient time nor choice for this, and the result will be an unsuitable product.

It is vital to compel scenarists to write scenarios evolving directly from the material; arguments that their artistic work will suffer from this are groundless: what is evidenced will be the production of a professional film studio and not amateur handicraft.

If film stories are only made to order, not arising from suitable material but only from the stories themselves, they will be exceptionally expensive, often artistically unsuccessful. Such an approach to business is unprofitable. It is vital for us to establish the economical production of a great quantity of films—hundred percenters, both in execution and in content.

6: The Training of the Actor

We know from an analysis of cinematic material that people performing organized, efficient work appear best on the screen. Remember the example of the stevedore carrying sacks onto a ship. Because he makes his movements so economically, deftly, and deliberately, because he spends many years at this business, this work appears exceptionally distinct on the screen, quickly and clearly comprehended by the viewer.

Only the filming of children and animal movement can compare with a demonstration of the labor processes of man, by virtue of its profound innocence, naturalness, and simplicity. Theatrical performance, actorship, is poor material for the celluloid; the reasons were explained in Chapter 2, concerning the material of the cinema. At the same time, we must film dramas, comedies, vaudeville films, because their production represents the fundamental section of the film industry. Apparently, it is possible to find appropriate methods of work in the fictional film when the filming of actors will provide completely satisfactory results. If, on the one hand, labor processes appear especially well, then, on the other hand, even the pure eccentrism of Chaplin comes out exceptionally cinematically.

What is the point?

The point is that one must construct the work of film actors so that it comprises the sum of organized movement, with "reliving" held to a minimum. Scenarios must express the reactions of the characters to what takes place, expressed by each person's treatment of objects and people through movement. This movement may be organized by the director, through a similar labor process. We have already discussed this both in the chapter on cinematic material and in the chapter on scenarios (Chapter 5). Our finest film actors are prepared at film schools. When they arrive at school, they try from the first to theatricalize—to transform themselves and to emote. In order to reeducate them, in order to make cinematographers of them, as distinguished from theatrical "sufferers"—that is, to make specialists in screen matters commanding a specific technique of them—it was necessary to compel them to perform a series of exercises for several years—to learn film-acting technique.

Our exercises, our training were conceived according to the fundamentals of those laws that we managed to extract from an analysis of the structure of the film, the camera, and the human mechanism of the actor. The fundamental exercises determine the structure of film-acting training and are the material of the present chapter. Say a person arrives for work at a film school. He is already thinking that he can perform separate episodes and scenes. How are they done? They are done by way of "reliving" and a free improvisation on the content of the episode. A person concentrates, tries to imagine himself as whatever he conceives, then begins to do everything necessary, as he imagines it, in whatever way it comes out for him. If it is given to a beginner to invent a task for himself, the task will invariably be complicated and confused. Only a heartrending dramatic scene and a complex comic episode will attract his attention. For beginning actors, elementary tasks are indispensable, and even if they are given to an accomplished theatrical worker, their performance in ninety-nine out of a hundred cases will be extremely unsatisfactory.

In the Academy of Art there was a professor of drawing named Chistyakov; he would show people through his mastery of the pencil that, essentially speaking, they did not know how to draw. And in actuality, he had them draw a pencil or a box from nature and later, with a ruler and plumb line in hand, demonstrated their complete incompetence in drawing technique.

In the same way, actors, having come to study our film work, cannot content themselves with such an elementary task as how to enter a room, take a chair, approach a window and open a transom. Ordinarily, such a task is done with a scornful derision—so easy and elementary does it seem. If you ask an actor to perform this task several times, you will see that it is performed variously, with different motions, and comes out sometimes better, sometimes worse.

How should the task be performed then?

First of all, the general task should be broken down into a series of elementary, separate smaller tasks.

A person enters a room—the first point of the problem.

A room may be entered in various ways (we begin the analysis with an already opened door).

Which hand holds the handle of the door? How best to hold the hand itself? Which leg enters the room first?

In which attitude will the body be?

What will the other hand be doing; in which position will it be? What is the head doing? (We will not, for the present, discuss the face, its function, its expression.)

All the questions need to be put to oneself, and for every indicated body part; for the entire body, corresponding attitudes must be found.

So far as we do not have in this étude the task for a manifestation of one or another type-image of an actor, to that extent the character of all these movements and body-attitudes must be calculated on the basis of the complete conception and economy of the given labor process.

The more complex work will be done in due regard of the image, when the character of the movement will determine the outlined nature of the given role. Thus, all the minutest details must be taken into consideration. But, perhaps, this is indispensable only as a point of departure. By no means. What follows will equally demand the most exact calculation and regard of the entire action. Only then will the necessary precision result, the necessary conviction of the actor's work, linked to the clear and simple education of the viewer.

We investigate our task further. A person takes a first step. How is it taken? In what position are all the articulated parts of the person? How does a hand detach itself from the door handle or how does it shut the door? What position of the body is most convenient and most necessary for the given task? What is the head doing, etc.? It will be further necessary to examine the room. When should it be examined? Immediately upon closing the door, or having taken several steps? If one should take several steps, how should they be taken and for what distance? How many steps should one take, on which foot should one start? And what are the body, the hands, the head doing? The actor must answer all these questions himself, or receive the answers from the director. Every separate problem must be painstakingly researched, performed many times, until the actor learns to accomplish precisely what is required in perfect form.

How should the room be examined?

Clearly, it is possible to turn one's head, creating the appearance that you are looking around the room, but the sense achieved by this is minimal. It is vital to mark precisely where, at which points, in what successive order, the eyes of the person working will scan. But is a room examined by the eyes alone? Is it not preferable to include the movement of the head to make the work of the eyes easier? And how is the person standing at this time? On which leg is his weight placed?

Perhaps on both. And if on one, then the second is free—in a normal or tensed condition; that is, is it on the toes, or the side of the shoe, or the heel? If the weight is on both legs, is it actually distributed evenly, or is it possible to lift one foot from the ground? What are the hands doing? What is the body doing? How, later, will a chair be sought; how will the actor pick it up; which part will he touch? How will he carry it? And so on, and so on—to calculate, to measure, to perform, until everything is thoroughly executed.

Training for such problems—so that they are exactly and accurately performed—must take up all the beginning hours of the training of the film actor. Exercises must be conceived either independently, or the trainer ought to devise them. I cite yet another typical exercise in this plan (I give it in general terms; the actor himself must break down the whole into its component parts).

A person enters his own room, straightens it up, brews some tea, drinks it, lies down to sleep. The actor fulfills such an exercise independently, devising what he will be doing, and independently establishes all the separate moments of the task. Only after he factually calculates everything and learns to accomplish it both accurately and thoroughly can he perform an étude before the instructor.

Generally, for the accomplishment of these exercises, there will not be enough of the necessary objects either in the home or in the classroom. The actor will have to work with imaginary objects, exceedingly useful for his education.

Ask someone to drink from an imaginary glass, and then to place it on a table. You will observe from the fingers of the drinking person that the glass has neither dimension nor form. And it is placed on the table as if it were made not of glass but of rags.

Try to speak into an imaginary telephone or to write with an imaginary pencil. You will squeeze your hand into a fist as far as it will go, as if there is nothing within it, and you will trace across the paper with your fingers, not taking into account the possible length of the pencil. Simultaneously with such exercises, it is vital to train actors on plot-less precise problems.

Let us say that the actor must climb over a pile of obstacles, and then sit down on a chair or fall. Every move of every limb, determined in advance by the director, constitutes, of itself, the overcoming of technical difficulties—is not at once apparent and must be completely learned, rehearsed. Concentrating on the performance of movements complex and difficult to fulfill, the actor markedly strengthens his technique after ten such assignments.

When the elementary precision of the actor is achieved, it is best to go on to the time element in his work, to metrics and rhythm. It is insufficient to perform precise and measured movements; it is necessary to be able to do them in time. Duration is movement; and time, that which goes toward its fulfillment—both of them must fit into a fundamental metrical rhythm. Very often études that are well-planned in movement appear synthetic, unconvincing. This happens due to an incorrect tempo of movement and an incorrect relationship of the duration of separate manipulations—that is, an uncalculated meter and rhythm of action. Training must be begun with the timing of the étude in mind.

The metronome counts metrical units while the actor performs each movement, according to a prearranged plan, in required tempo. The basic count is the same as in music: either two-four or three-four time, or a combination of the two. Likewise, as in music, three-four metrical time more closely fits lyrical themes (the waltz), two-four, bold, energetic tempos (the march). The most convenient measure for work in études is four-four. Without the introduction of metrical measurement of action, it will invariably be unclear and diffuse. Imagine for yourself the distance from one place to another, let us say from Moscow to Leningrad. For us the conception of the distance will be clear only because we recognize the changing units of space—kilometers; if there were no measure of the space, there would be no conception of it. Large towns between two major cities help better to establish in our senses the measuring of space. The same also with the measurement of time in the work of the film actor: the duration of an étude can be broken down into basic units of measure. Just as towns along the way help us better to understand the sections of space in the example of Moscow and Leningrad, so the accented powerful fourths set off one measure of the movement from another. The count is measured thus: one, two, three, four, etc. The first fourth is stressed, the basic movements are made on it, the energetic key movements. Evenly repeated one after another, even if by skipped beats, such movements will be comprehended by the viewer calmly, as in the basic tempo of the étude. If the required movement is sharply accented, unexpected, and must be so because of the timing (syncopation), then the desired result of unexpectedness will be attained. Of course it is possible to construct wholly syncopated études. One must warn musicians that we take from music its elementary meter and rhythm for completely understandable reasons and employ these ideas in the most simple, the most intelligible forms. When we have to deal with the category of space, we study space on the basis of plastic-viewing principles. When we deal with the category of time, we must naturally employ the method of temporal art—inasmuch as film-art is young, inasmuch as we use this material as simplified and elementary.

After the training actor familiarizes himself with temporal work through a series of exercises, it is necessary to move on to the notation of movement and to rhythmical training. Imagine that your hand is extended forward and outstretched to the left, the fingers holding a glass; you have to move your hand far to the right and place the glass on the table, and after that to place the hand in your pocket.

The étude is conducted in a four-four count. If the movement is to be conducted by counts, let us say—on the first fourth of the first measure, the hand is brought to the right; on the second fourth of the second measure, the hand puts down the glass; and on the first fourth of the third measure, the hand is put into the pocket—then this does not mean that the duration of the movements will be taken into consideration. Let us take the first measure: the hand movement can take up the whole measure, or three fourths, or two to two and a half, or two and an eighth, etc.

The consideration of the timing of movement in an already calculated temporal order of movement will be the next stage of the rhythm-training of the actor. The system permits the exact notation of movement using notational signs, as in music. Example. First measure: hand with glass moves right (). Second measure: hand puts down glass (). Third measure: hand directed toward pocket ().

In the first measure, the movement of the hand occurs in three-quarter time; in the second, one eighth (of a four-part measure); in the third, two quarters (the rests not noted). For the work of each movement a temporal count is indispensable. In complex études the understanding for everyone of parallel movements, of their rhythmical order, is most difficult without being accustomed to it, and it is necessary to practice this to the point the skill is acquired to perform the movements according to the written notations, in the same way that a musician plays by notes—almost unconsciously.

Along with the enumeration of exercises of elementary problems, it is necessary to create complexities for the sake of exactness, to perform with a pair or with several people, and to introduce into these the primary elements of the stresses (a stress is explained in detail: the alternation of strong and weak, energetic and weakened movements—will be discussed later). Wrestling and fighting are very helpful in learning the technique of the étude—best of all when actors who are familiar with acrobatics, boxing, and gymnastics perform the études. Sport and the practice of physical discipline are vital for each film actor to learn and to try to be familiar with; instruction in them in schools is obligatory, but they must be taught specially, not in their pure form, but as applicable to film in consideration of the wide utilization of the accumulated training and knowledge.

Even when disciplined actors are given the assignment of a fight, even in the beginning, the études end up in chaotic muddles of movement. One cannot discern who is victorious at a given moment and who is defeated. The impression of an energetic fight does not result, the étude looks maudlin, because the actors are afraid to upstage each other, or else, in a senseless rage, to injure each other, with no result. A diagram of the increases of effort of the participants must be formulated. Breaking down an entire étude into its periods, it is crucial to establish when A is stronger than B, when their strength is equal and when one overcomes the other by a series of strong movements. Having formulated a scheme, each movement, each shifting of weight, each grappling must be analyzed in its minutest detail, to learn to perform everything slowly and then subsequently to perform everything at the normal speed.

At the same time, training in falling is practiced, for which great experience and skill are needed.

One ought to move on to work with one's face with great care. Cinema does not tolerate emphatic, crude work with the face; theatrical technique is not applicable to the screen, because the radius of movement on the stage is too great. On the screen the most seemingly unnoticeable changes of the face become too crude—the viewer will not believe in such acting. The face is trained in a series of exercises with a mandatory regard of the metrical and rhythmical timing of the work. The face may change as a result of the work of the forehead, the brows, eyes, nose, cheeks, lips, lower jaw. The forehead can be normal, furrowed, raised; the brows—likewise; eyes normal, closed, half-closed, opened, opened wide, turned right, left, up, down. The nose can be wrinkled, cheeks puffed out and sucked in, lips and mouth clenched, opened, half-opened, turned up (laughter), turned down; the lower jaw can be energetically thrust forward, can be moved right and left. In general, for the work of the face and all the parts of a human being, the system of Delsarte is very useful, but only as an inventory of the possible changes in the human mechanism, and not as a method of acting.

An actor's part in this system is unacceptable, but the basic purpose of the system of classifying all the bodily movements as normal, eccentric, and concentric, and the combination of these, must be learned by the film actor.

Let us return to the exercises for the face.

Here is an example of an étude:

(1) Face normal; (2) eyes squinting, move to the right; (3) pause; (4) forehead and brows frown; (5) lower jaw moves forward; (6) eyes abruptly shift to the right; (7) lower jaw to the left; (8) pause; (9) face

normal, but the eyes remain in the previous position; (10) eyes open wide, simultaneously the mouth half-opens, etc.

With such a problem, it is crucial to put it to a count, to establish the duration of each position, the duration of arriving at that position, and the duration of doing it. Conscientious training of the face will rapidly train the actor to master it completely, so that he will be able to execute any of his own or the director's assignments. Many special exercises for the eyes exist; for example, it is very difficult for them to move evenly along a horizontal line right and left; so as to accomplish a smooth motion, one must hold a pencil in one's outstretched arm and look at it constantly and move it before oneself, parallel to the floor. Such an exercise quickly accustoms the eyes to operate smoothly, which has much better results on the screen than jerky, abrupt movements (unless they are specifically required, of course).

Apart from the fact that each group of the parts of the human body can be normal, concentric, and eccentric, the entire human mechanism tends either to greater concentricity or eccentricity during work; that is, the whole body somehow gathers itself, coils itself, uncoils itself. Clear views of this coiling and uncoiling happen seldom; more often, these processes occur with mixtures, transgressions, and predominance of a tendency in either one or the other direction. For clear as well as "hybrid" coiling and uncoiling, a series of études is performed, with and without themes. Example: the directors are given a scheme—six measures of a gradually unwinding resolving nature, six measures of winding, three measures of unwinding, one measure of winding, one measure of unwinding, etc., while the learner must invent a theme for this design, so that the projected processes would exactly fit the content, the subject. Into these very exercises the consideration of the performance platform is included—the raising and lowering of the body working in relationship to the floor.

Now let us move on to the most important aspect of the training of the technique of the actor—to the spatial, metric web, and to the work along the fundamental axes of all the parts of the human organism. In the chapter (2) on the material of cinema we already touched on this question; it is vital to repeat it in even greater detail. Let us begin with the metric web.

Imagine for yourself a rectangular screen. Its proportions are invariable, its sides have the same relationship of length. The motion of light and shadow of the cinematic action takes place on this screen surface. Everything that occurs on the screen is read by the viewer's eyes, somehow is absorbed into his consciousness, and, moreover, sometimes this process occurs easily, without the expenditure of excessive strain, sometimes with difficulty, forcing the viewer to strain, to perceive what occurs with difficulty. Taking into account the fixed proportions of the screen, the length of the projected pieces, and the perceptual capacity of the viewer, it is apparent that it is possible to establish laws, according to which one can construct a simple and clear motion of objects and actors in the cinema. Imagine that the screen is an unfilled, empty white rectangle. The paths of possible movement across the screen can be recorded by lines (of direction or movement). If we chart by lines a chaotic, spontaneous action on the screen, it is easy to see that confused, diverse lines will reach the consciousness of the viewer with great difficulty. If the action takes place, say, along one line (of action), if it can be schematically conceived in terms of some characteristic, it will then be perceived by the viewer substantially more easily. Further, when the line of action is completely readable, then its arrangement on the screen will be particularly distinct. Then it will be arranged in the screen-space so that its place of location will be easily determined by those who determine the form of the screen-space by its borders. If a line is parallel to the lower or upper sides of the screen and perpendicular to the right and left, obviously the position of this line will be distinct for the viewer. If we begin to rotate the line slowly and carefully on the screen surface, its perception by the viewer will be made more complicated. The more imperceptibly we shift (or tilt) the line, the more difficult it is to understand how it is situated; the more the incline of the line is distinct, the easier the reading of it by the viewer will be.

Consequently, if we film a line of concrete action—simply arranged on the screen, its mastering by a spectator will make use of the film-demonstration significantly less than if it were to be a little tilted. That is why less footage is needed for pieces of an industrial character or architectural construction than a complicated rural scene—which, if it is to be well observed, must be shown longer.

If one records the lines of movement of an ordinary actor on the screen, the result is chaotic; if one records deliberate organized work, the result is a strict design of lines, which is read much more easily than the previous confused one.

Thus, if movements take place on the screen (to put it primitively) parallel to one pair of the screen sides and perpendicular to the other, then these movements will be more clear, more easily perceived by the viewer.

If there is even a negligible deviation in the movement, the apprehension of the viewer will be complicated. If the movement diverges significantly, for example, to an angle of 45 degrees, then once again it will be easy for the viewer to perceive it.

If necessary movements within the surroundings and the combination of surroundings are eccentric, these complex movements must be somehow written in, sketched in along with the basic straight lines. On the screen an imaginary web somehow results, and it is along it that one must move during the elementary action, while during the complex action, crooked movements must be situated into the fundamental parallel and perpendicular divisions.

This imaginary web on the screen is termed by us the metrical spatial web.

In consideration of this, the work of the film actor must be constructed with the distinction that the actor moves not along the surface of the screen, but in a three-dimensional space in the studio or outdoors. The space of his action represents a pyramid (however abstract), the apex of which rests against the center of the lens of the camera. Thus, the two-dimensional web must transform itself for the actor into a three-dimensional one, situated in the pyramidal space of action. Consequently, the actor will move somehow in the cubic space, along the planes of the grid immediately ahead of him, along the grid on the floor, and along the grid alongside him (this is in the event of the actor standing facing the camera). The continuation of the transection of the lines of all the three surfaces of these grids creates the cubic space of the shot's action; while the cubic space is situated in the pyramid, determined by the angle of the lens of the filming camera.

Let us move on to the *axes* of movement.

It would appear that though a person has the ability to move his articulated body as he chooses, to account for these movements seems impossible. We consider it, and it appears that such is not the case. A space can be measured in three dimensions—length, width, and depth; consequently, the movement of each joint (part of the body) occurs along three basic axes: to the right and left, along the horizontal; upward and downward, along the vertical; and along the transverse, to the sides. Example: the movement of the head: (1) along the first axis—the gesture corresponding to doubt or reproach (what! what!).

All the remaining movements of this part of the body will be combinations of the three fundamental axes. No other movements are possible.

Let us formulate a table of movement along the axes of the principle parts of the human body:

The actor must construct his work along the basic axes or in terms of their combinations, and to arrange them in the space within the cubic space. Let us take for an example the movement of the waist along Axis No. 2.

In the outline we see that this will be the inclination of the entire body from the waist forward and backward. Which positions of the body, moving along the second axis, will be the most distinct? Those which occupy the simple, clearly legible positions on the screen-surface, in the direction of the movement—that is, the clearly straightforward position of a person, a clear inclination of the body, in an

Body Part	*Axis No. 1*	*Axis No. 2*	*Axis No. 3*
1. Eyes	Right, left	Upward, downward	None, there is a combination of No. 1 and No. 2, a rotating movement
2. Head	Right, left	Upward, downward	None
3. Neck	Negation	Affirmation	Doubt
4. Clavicle (collar bone)	Movement of the shoulder forward and backward	None	Upward, downward
5. Shoulder (the arm from shoulder to hand)	Rotation of entire arm	Forward (in front of oneself), backward (away from oneself)	At the side, away from the side
6. Elbow (the arm from elbow to hand)	Rotation (turning a key in a lock)	Toward oneself	At the side, away from the side
7. Hand	None	Toward oneself	To the side
8. Waist	Turning of the body	Tilting the body forward and backward	Tilting the body to the side
9. Hip	Turning the entire leg (rotation)	Jeté (great leap) forward, backward	Jeté (great leap) to the side
10. Knee	Rotation	Forward, backward	None
11. Foot	Turned inward, outward	Extended and gathered, raising	Foot turned under (as if ankle twisted), inward, outward

upright-position of the body and legs in relationship to the floor. The intermediate positions of the body will be difficult for viewers to perceive and will require holding the image longer on the screen.

Experience has shown that the better an actor works, the more complete his technique, the more intricately he can construct his movements. The good actor will come to terms with the most complete combinations of axes and the most minor inclinations and angles of the metrical web. The most difficult is to move from one position into another; here is where the highly developed technique of the film actor is needed. Therefore, if the director must work with weak technical material, he must use it primitively, to require that movement be along the lines of the metrical web. If the actor is well trained, he can perform the most minute, the slightest movements to perfection, and, most importantly, will be able to move from one position to another with perfection. It is in this that the virtuosity of his technique will be shown.

One is categorically cautioned against having inexperienced people perform complex roles—the result is abominable; while working along simple plans, all the characters will appear well, convincingly, and comprehensibly to those working. The path toward perfection and the attainment of a broad range—great potentials in screen movement—lie in the training by études, building on the axes of movement and the web.

Needless to say, while in production one cannot think about this method; it is vital that in schooling it has been absorbed into the flesh and blood, so that the actor works unconsciously, precisely, and clearly, so that he can move differently. Dilettantes will give the impression of jerking marionettes, who are categorically unacceptable for the screen, which requires foremost of all—reality and simplicity.

After the axial training, a consideration of stress follows, the shift from high-energy movements to slack and weak movements. The human body consists of flesh and bones; they have weight, are pulled to earth, and if the energy level slackens, the human being falls. The more easily man overcomes gravity, the more energy he possesses. Movements can be energetic, strong, light, and weak.

Imagine that you are holding a dumbbell; the more easily you thrust your arm upward, the more strength you possess. The more slowly the arm is raised, the more the weight will be demonstrated.

Conversely: the greater the weight, the more quickly the arm falls downward; the more slowly it is lowered, the stronger the man. Consequently, slower movements downward and quicker movements upward are indications of the presence of energy; changes in the tempo of upward movements toward slowness and downward movements toward rapidity demonstrate a slackening of energy. A rapid fall of a person and a slow getting up signify weakness.

A surplus of energy generally coincides with a propensity toward extroversion, the undertaking of eccentric positions; a fall, by contrast, results in introversion, in concentricity.

Exercises in "heaviness and lightness," that is, in the raising and lowering of the energy level, are especially difficult and at the same time indispensable, because they train the actor to an ultimate control of his body.

Everything analyzed to this point is summarized in special exercises which may be termed the "score" (in the musical sense) of the action. In the beginning the études are played individually according to the scores, then are done in pairs, threes, etc. The score—that is, the exact plan given to the director—the scheme of the action for each variation of movement, has its own line. The outline of the basic movements is given along this line. All the lines correspond to each other, while the job of the actor is to invent a story to go with them, to calculate the logically required number of lines for the outline.

In such an étude it is necessary to have a line of movement and rhythm in which the temporal aspect of the étude is clearly worked out, the order established, and the duration of all movements determined in advance.

The second line is the plastic one, the recording of movements is achieved by charting the basic positions, notation of the axes or the combinations of them, notation of the direction across the web.

The third line is curtailment or development, with or without complications. In this line the number of measures of one or another condition and their sequence one after another is determined.

The fourth line is a calculation of the raising and lowering of the body in relation to the floor and the performance platform on the floor.

The fifth line is a calculation of intensity, how the energy level is raised and lowered, at which moment comes the turn in the situation, how the change from maximum to minimum emphasis occurs.

Each line has its own conditions of appearance, its own imprint. The result is something approaching musical notation, by which one can see what happens in each measure of action along each line.

This work is the most interesting, giving the actor a maximum of technical virtuosity and training him to be able to control himself completely, giving a good account of himself in everything he does. Of course, these exercises are vital only for training.

The enumerated training of the outward technique of the actor must be supplemented by a parallel study of the human reflexes of behavior. But an analysis of this independent discipline of learning, I repeat, ought not to lead one to fear that the stated training might bring one to unnecessary schematization, harshness of acting before the motion picture camera. One need not regard the system as a style, one need not permit needless awkwardness or crudeness in the work. One ought to work gently, calmly, and—most important of all—freely and assuredly.

After the entire course of study is completed, the required confidence will ensue in the actor in his movements, his relationship to natural simplicity. Chaos, which is disorganized, muddled, confused work, will be done away with, replaced by expressive clarity, assuredness, which is demonstrated to the entire world by Chaplin, Lon Chaney, Adolphe Menjou, Mary Pickford, and other first-rate actors.

7: In Production

It is one thing to work experimentally in school, another to go into production. Without practical shooting sessions, without experiments on the set itself, there cannot be complete perfection. Only through testing one's knowledge by experience, supplementing it, searching for new methods of work, is it possible to advance, to develop film-culture. The principal thing is that theoretically one cannot calculate everything, for practice sometimes shatters the core of theoretical postulations, if a mistake has been permitted in them

There are errors in preliminary estimates, which can be revealed only in production.

How, then, must work be conducted?

Before all else, there must be nothing hack, nothing accidental and thoughtless. A firm production plan must be formulated for the shooting of a film, the number of shooting days set, the scenario broken down to the most minute detail, the budget drawn up, etc.

The guarantee of the success of a future film lies in the correct organization of shooting and the well-considered, concise approach of the director. Without a good administrator, supplied with efficient assistants, the success of a film will not be assured.

One cannot work with accidentally chosen people: all members of the production crew must be familiar with one another, must agree, must know the virtues and peculiarities of each person. There cannot be a single filming session that is not carefully organized beforehand. The director must know everything in advance and write down his demands for his assistants exactly.

I remember how practicably the basic rules of shooting evolved for us, which we could not realize in any way beforehand. Approaching the work, we carefully analyzed the scenario, determined the position of each shot, and knew exactly what was to occur in each shot. The scenarios were constructed by montage. To economize on film stock and time, only those shots were taken that were established in the plan. It was apparent that chance, new ideas, unexpected material, the absence of an exact montage list will disrupt the montage of the film unless there is a surplus of material. If the scenario has a long-shot, cutting to a series of close-ups, then cutting in again, it is crucial to shoot the same action in the long-shot as in the close-ups. One cannot rely solely on long-shots; one can never be guaranteed against lapses in action or in time. It is most desirable for the master shots to have uninterrupted continuity, and to shoot the details from various points of view, with the close-ups afterwards, or simultaneously (if the light permits).

While editing, the director must have an unlimited amount of material; the more there is the better the film will turn out; but this material must be as diverse as possible. One ought to strive for the minimal amount of duplications, repeats; it is vital to expend all the film stock, all one's time, all one's energy on the shooting of *variations.*

Generally, the director reads the scene to the actors, they rehearse a little, and then the cameraman films it. Let us say the first take is poor. The director comments, points out shortcomings, and the shooting is resumed. Such a procedure may be repeated many times, the actors change their work each time, move chaotically and in an undetermined tempo.

In the result—at the time of cutting—uniform pieces of takes of unorganized acting from one point of view will lie before the director. To be sure, it is possible to select the best from these pieces, but time and film expended on this achievement of a highly dubious result will be justified neither artistically nor commercially. In fact, instances frequently occur when, during a screening of the rushes, one cannot distinguish one take from another, so deceptive to the eye is the actor's work. And do not instances occur when one scene is shot fifty times from one point of view, and later in seeing the rushes one realizes that it would have been better to set the camera up elsewhere? A discovery often occurs late, and there are no opportunities for reshooting. It is not only in our country that they shoot the same thing so rashly; I have heard accounts from authoritative filmmakers about foreign film work: one of them saw how an ordinary scene of an actor creeping along a wall was reshot an endless number of times. If one sets and rehearses every movement of an actor until such time that one gets precisely what is wanted, the shooting results will be far more productive. It is possible and necessary to reshoot a scene once, two times, but only after every detail down to the minutest is absolutely, precisely rehearsed. From what has been said it does not follow that one ought not use a lot of film in shooting—the spoilage is bound to be very great—but one ought to shoot variations of calculated, tightly reasoned scenes, repeats, after all, being superfluous. The greater the director's choice of various pieces in editing, the greater the sources of success with the spectator. For some reason, everyone reacts to the scrupulously reasoned rehearsal with scorn. It appears that this arises from the fact that few people know how to work with precision. When in the beginning we spent half the shooting day on rehearsals at our studio, the studio head looked upon us as mad wastrels and artistic ignoramuses. The results forced everyone to become convinced in the rightness of our method of work: the films turned out to be under budget and of high artistic quality. The exact staging of every minute movement of the actor provides unlimited possibilities of montage. The fact is that if the actors performed the same scene with variations during several shooting sessions, with the same movements, then matching the pieces shot from different points of view would become impossible, the action would not coincide. And the principal expression, the main effect of montage, is the absolute concision of movement. It sometimes becomes necessary to show one movement shot at once from several points of view, to break it down into a series of movements. One can cut such a piece successfully only in the event of the consistency of the performance of this actor through all the pieces. True, there is another method: shooting with multiple cameras—a method that is too expensive and is sometimes impracticable from the standpoint of technical considerations (either lights cannot be placed for simultaneous shooting from various points of view, or space prohibits this).

It is most desirable to shoot in this way:

1. The director and the actor determine the general character of the scene, indicating all movements.

2. The assistant director learns the scene from director and actor.

3. The director checks and finally polishes the scene.

4. Shooting.

If the scale of the shooting permits and if the director has sufficient assistants, whom he fully trusts artistically, it is advantageous to set several parallel scenes in different places of the shooting. With this method the director's head is not crammed with the process of the actor's learning, he does not lose a fresh outlook on the scene, and productiveness increases manyfold.

In *The Death Ray* (1925) we were able to do mass scenes inexpensively and artistically successfully; we staged them on the grounds of the former Agricultural Exhibition. The shooting locations were surveyed with the cameraman, Levitsky, and the designer, Pudovkin; the shots were determined exactly, photographed with a still camera and sketched. At home I put together the plan of the mass scenes for each shot, mustered all my assistants and gave each a not too large assignment, having thoroughly indicated what each must do with his people, vehicles, horses in "shot No. such-and-such," when to send them out, and so on. The result was significant: within three days enormous mass scenes were shot without any excess commotion and strain, with high quality, dispatch, and economy.

The better such means of working are, the more senseless the director's shouting and fussing during the shooting, with his tongue hanging out, madly dashing about, making the lighting technicians nervous, while the actors stand around waiting for no reason.

Of course, apart from the budget itself, there are chance unpredictabilities during the shooting: either something does not work or a new thought comes into the director's head, or something unexpected is discovered, material unaccounted for earlier. In such an instance, one cannot but deviate from the plan—on the contrary: every chance occurrence, every new discovery, every opportunity to enrich the shooting material must be used. In such an instance, the director must quickly orient himself to exploit more fully and better the newly discovered material.

The greater the opportunity for the replenishment of the material for shooting, the easier the direction, the better the film comes out. It is more difficult to work with limited material. The experience of working with limited material was put into practice in filming *By the Law*, in which three characters perform, during five reels of the film (five people perform in only the first reel), and everything takes place in one room—a single set. The material for the shooting of this film was extremely circumscribed; it was vital only to perfect it thoroughly, so that the viewer's attention would be sustained, undiminished until the final reel. For this successful experience, a markedly greater degree of working energy within the group involved in the shooting was required—no less than on a production of an enormous film with dozens of sets and crowd scenes. All our experience, all our knowledge had to be marshaled without limit to overcome the restricted material. One cannot work in this manner all the time—the exhaustion of the film company is greater than can be justified; therefore it is better to have the opportunity to shoot a great quantity of varied material.

One can formulate an axiom: the greater the experience of the master director and the film company, the more restricted it is possible for the film material to be; the more inexperienced the company, the greater the filmic options must be that are to be afforded it.

At present I am intensely concerned with something else—artistic-economic experiment. The point is that our standard, middle-grade films are shot over many months and cost a great deal, while being mediocre in their artistic quality. This happens because the shooting is improperly organized, because the directors do not fully use the help of assistants and do not work with a specially trained acting staff. I strive to emphasize that with proper organization of the shooting a qualified director with experienced assistants, cameramen, set designers, and a harmoniously working group of actors can shorten by seventy-five percent the estimated shooting schedule without lowering the artistic quality of the completed film.

Try to keep an exact shooting diary: you will observe how much time and energy is expended needlessly. True, very often the organization of the film studio becomes the principal hindrance, and not the organization of the film unit. At the same time, experience has proved the truth, it would appear—a paradoxical conclusion: the more precisely the director works with the company, the more thoroughly he rehearses and calculates everything, the more quickly the shooting of the film will be completed.

In conclusion, I must say a few words about the making of non-fictional films, about the newsreel. The foundation of cinematography is the montage of real material—to speak clearly and distinctly in favor of the non-fictional. We know that actual things come out most successfully as a counterbalance to the artistic-fictional. Regrettably, insufficient attention almost everywhere is paid to the filming of newsreels. Almost no type of film exists that could be viewed with such genuine, real interest, comparable to a large fictional film production. Still, during recent years there were a few films that could fully contend with the artistic ones.

Now, the struggle for the non-fictional film is no longer necessary; most now believe in its utility, indispensability, and the genuineness of its interest. The time for agitation has passed; it is necessary to approach the *study* of non-fictional films fully. It is necessary to throw the finest working efforts into the non-fictional film: the finest directors, the best cameramen, the best editors.

The root error is in the fact that the shooting of newsreels is considered inexpensive. This assumption is false: a good newsreel is expensive, not cheaper but more expensive than fictional films.

The organization of the non-fictional film studio, the travel, the equipment, the changing of location, and the accompanying technical gear are extremely complicated and costly. The main obstacle to the development of such shooting is the fact that cinematography is still technically weak. It was only a few years ago that the smaller, perfected models of motion picture cameras for newsreels were built. Even now in the USSR we do not have a single cameraman for the Eyemo, which is one of the finest present-day newsreel cameras. Not having our own film manufacturing plants, we do not have the opportunity to get the most sensitive stock. To order it from abroad is impossible—it can only be preserved a few months—while the most sensitive sorts of raw film can be prepared only for the time of the actual shooting and require immediate use. Moreover, without highly sensitive film stock a whole host of the most important subjects at night or in poorly lit buildings are not possible to film. It is true, we have at our disposal light-sensitive (fast) lenses, such as the "Plasmat" of Dr. Rudolph,* with light strengths of f1 and f2, but all the same, such a lens without sensitive film is not enough. Fast lenses for the most part produce a fuzzy image, lacking in depth of field and clarity; once more we are dealing with the technical inadequacy of the cinema. Working with portable lights cannot be considered satisfactory for newsreels either, simply because one cannot shoot inconspicuously with such equipment.

In buildings not adapted for filming it is impossible to shoot everything happening because there is no place to step back: the angle of vision of perception of the eye of the lens requires considerable "stepping-back" from what is to be photographed. The film camera "perceives" from a different angle of vision from that of our eyes. The most wide-angle lens from among those known to us is the "Takhar," with a focal length of 28 mm, but I do not know whether one of our newsreel cameramen has it.

Until such time as we find the forms of regular structures for non-fictional films, until light-sensitive film stock is widely available, until we have economical, portable lights—until that time, non-fictional films will not really develop.

Ideologues of the non-fictional film!—give up convincing yourselves of the correctness of your viewpoints: they are indisputable. Create or point out methods of creating genuine, exciting newsreels. Organize a film studio, special newsreel equipment and film stock, achieve new technical discoveries—an advancement of cinematog-

* Dr. Paul Rudolph (1858–1935) was the designer of the first anastigmat lens for the German firm, Zeiss, in 1895.

raphy. When it is possible to film easily and comfortably, without having to consider either the location, or the light conditions, then the authentic flowering of the non-fictional film will take place, depicting our environment, our construction, our land.

SELECTED ESSAYS

AMERICANITIS

STARTING in 1914 and going on to the present (1922), anyone who systematically frequents film theaters, viewing all the films that are released from Russian as well as foreign studios, anyone who has noticed which films cause the audience to react to cinematic action, would conclude the following:

1. Foreign films appeal more than Russian ones.

2. Of the foreign films, all the American ones and detective stories appeal most.

The public especially "feels" American films. When there is a clever maneuver by the hero, a desperate pursuit, a bold struggle, there is such excited whistling, howling, whooping, and intensity that interested figures leap from their seats, so as to see the gripping action better.

Both superficial people and deep-thinking officials get equally frightened by "Americanitis" and "detectivitis" in the cinema and explain the success of the particular films by the extraordinary decadence and poor "tastes" of the youth and the public of the third balcony.

Undeniably, literary subjects are irrelevant for them, and the decadence of the public is not worth discussing.

It is crucial in these observations to direct one's center of attention to the people of the third balcony, because the majority of the public in the more expensive seats goes to the movies out of psychopathological or hysterical impulses.

The cinema has never had more subtle artistic constructions and complex "investigations," which would be incomprehensible to a less cultured public, while a reaction to more basic primitive moments of impression is much more vivid to an audience of average sensibility; and it is by far the more interesting in the current epoch.

In detective literature, and more so in the American detective scenario, the fundamental element of the plot is an intensity in the development of action, the dynamic of construction—*and for the cinema there is no more harmful expression of literariness than psychologism, i.e., the externally actionless of a given plot.*

The success of American motion pictures lies in the greatest common measure of film-ness, in the presence of maximum movement and in primitive heroism, in an organic relationship to contemporaneity.

Secondly, due to conditions of life in their country and their particular commercial methods, Americans are able to show more plot in a film of limited length and strive to attain the greatest number of scenes and the greatest impression with the least expenditure of film stock.

It is clear that in this case the length of footage of individual scenes, from which any long motion picture is assembled, is reduced to a minimum, and thus the scenes of an American film succeed one another more often than those in a Russian one.

Attempting, as much as possible, to shorten the length of each component part of a film, the length of each separate piece shot from a single set-up, the Americans discovered a simple method of simply solving the complexity of scenes by shooting only that element of movement without which at any given moment a necessary vital action could not occur; and the camera is placed in such a perspective on nature that the theme of a given movement itself reaches, and is cognized by, the viewer in the quickest, simplest, and most comprehensible form. (The close-up—a separate shot of the film.)

Thus the number of component parts in an American film, due to the method of shooting each separate scene in a whole sequence of component moments, becomes still greater.

Studying American films and comparing our observations with unsuccessful attempts in films shot by Russian directors who were using methods more familiar to us and seeking greater "film-ness," rather than the perpetuation of "theatricality," one unwillingly credits a certain stimulating power to films assembled consciously from a combination of sequences of changing scenes. The cinema is unable to record every separate scene (in one piece). The secret of mastery over cinematic material—the essence of cinematography—lies in its composition, the alternation of photographed pieces. In the main, for the organization of impressions, what is important is not what is shot in a given piece, but how the pieces in a film succeed one another, how they are structured.

We must seek the organization of cinematography not in the limitations of the exposed shot, but in the alternation of these shots.

So as to clarify the meaning of the aforesaid, let us point out that in the case of the construction of any material, the crucial moment is the organizational moment, during which the relationship of parts to the material and their organic, spatial, and temporal connections are revealed. The juxtaposition and interrelationship of various elements much more vividly and more convincingly expresses essence and meaning—as with each separate element, so with the whole assemblage.

Likewise with film, in the combination of exposed pieces, what is important is the dependency relationship of the first exposed piece to the second, and this dependency is the principal constructive moment in the building of a motion picture.

What is vital to note is that in the process of one's absorption in film work on the fundamentals of expression of its essence in the alternation of shot pieces, the first postulate derived from American films was often forgotten: the concretion of a necessary movement into a separate shot and the assemblage into one scene of these concretely expressed pieces, played out before the camera. This has an extraordinary significance for the production of an ordered cinematic construction.

The particular method is technically called shooting by the American format, while the joining of the pieces, assembled into a motion picture, is film editing.

Authentic cinema is the montage of American formats, and the essence of the cinema, its method of achieving maximal impression, is montage.

Since the sphere of these analyses of the cinema is derived from the dissection of American motion pictures, it is of course the case that these films are like "classics" for beginners in film, and hence, our opponents label research in the cinema by the word "anti-artistic," which to them means—"Americanitis."

[1922]

THE QUESTION OF THE FILM REPERTOIRE (In a Laboratory Setting)

SIMPLE TRUTHS: (1) the cinema must be active; (2) the cinematic material must be photogenic. The cinema is a moving photograph on separate frames, edited into a single whole. An organized event, in movement, as with plastic forms, turns out well; while a disorganized event turns out badly. A good piece of film educates the viewer. If we take a film perfectly well worked out ideologically and produce it poorly from the standpoint of form, then, despite its ideological skill, it will turn out to be a counterrevolutionary film.

The literary material of cinematography falls into three basic categories: (1) historical films; (2) contemporary films; (3) films of the future.

Historical films use anti-photogenic material in about ninety percent of such films. The external elements of any historical event are incomparably poorer in emotionally moving material than the elements of contemporary life. Let us take as an example, the methods of modern transportation, modern firearms, etc. All these produce a far greater range of possibilities for the dynamic construction of montage. If the cinematographic theme is not active, it is an obvious example of the misconception and misuse of the capabilities of cinema—consequently, what we have is material waste. That is how historical films may be assessed, as educational-historical texts, but not very important ones, for the modern viewer. It is possible to acquaint someone with the history of the Party, but to express the full power of communist work is feasible only in the contemporary repertoire. Historical events of the recent past are distinct by virtue of their remarkable non-photogenic quality. Nothing comes out more repulsively on the screen than the uniforms of a policeman or a tsarist officer. These costumes are absolutely uncinematic and the shots chosen and edited with them elicit, through their own disorder, a harmful psychological reaction from viewers.

The most interesting for our repertoire, of course, is the contemporary film. It must depict the genesis of our country, must depict the organization of the work of the proletariat, the new Soviet ambiance. By contrast with the documentary, the fictional film must not depict by merely recording actuality—it must infuse it as much as possible with the proletarian spirit.

All other attempts to depict individual dramas, garnished with their quotas of the rape of proletarian girls by White Army officers, are scarcely anything but the reflections of the counterrevolutionary, old, psychological cinema. It is not worthwhile to pay attention to their seemingly Soviet form: the form of contemporary films is usually anything but Soviet. This should be clear to everyone.

Now let us imagine that we will begin to solve major problems such as those just enumerated.

Suppose that we need to portray the birth and development of the railroad industry. We would have to arrive at the comparative method of the documentary film, which will be ponderous and convince very few, or depict our feelings about the railroad. To do this we would have to weave together a thousand different approaches, shoot, say, enormous first-class steam engines, their details and their movement. What exists in reality is very good, but, first of all, one ought to strive for better things, and secondly, what exists is completely inadequate for the cinema.

Seeking to build a completely modern Soviet cinema, our filmmakers use environmentally unphotogenic material. This happens because the filmmakers carry on the work under the inertia of the old cinematography, while the ideological laymen do not take into account the nature of cinematography. At present we are living through a transition period, which we must live through but need not show on the screen. A ramshackle peasant hut, a dour coachman, ancient houses, churches, slovenly landscapes, uncomfortable and needless uniforms are considered to be the creation of the contemporary Russian ambiance. This is counterfeit to the core, from the standpoint of formal essence, it is like the paintings of the "Itinerants." *

A transitional environment limits the dynamic possibilities for the construction of a scenario to an extraordinary extent. Individual dramas are not what we need; at the same time, we do not yet have the cinematically organized mass. Accordingly, it is important to seek—against the background of mass work—to produce temporarily individual work, at the same time deprived of individualism and expressing what we are unable to show with mass work. It is better to avoid the vividly expressive ambiant forms, in favor of building the forms of the film-story more imaginatively. This will produce the maximal action, will lend a filmic form, the conviction of which it is vital to use properly.

Let the organized people work, the people who are able to stand on their own feet, who are able to overcome obstacles that present themselves. This is much closer to the present mode of life. A properly functioning person, quickly oriented, vigorous and energetic, will teach us more important things and say greater things than a view of some wretched little hut, used as a fictional cabin. The image of energetically acting human beings will sooner force the viewers to live not in a rustic cabin, but in a fine new house, built by new people in an old place. In *The Death Ray*, for example, all the roles are directed toward the depiction of the labor of energetic people, to the end of the destruction of those obstacles interfering with the proper development

* A group of Russian painters in the second half of the nineteenth century, linked by social consciousness and extreme naturalism. R.L.

of things. And all this work is the expression of that will of that working mass which is the principal hero of the film. At the same time, there is a total renunciation of the minute atmospheric traits that are typically ours, because they are not the point. The main point is not the poor shoes of the worker and not his dismal shirt, but rather his energy and his labor. And as far as the uncomfortable footwear, the uncomfortable clothing, the uncomfortable living quarters are concerned, we are obliged to change them for the best possible. To use these, still not replaced, objects and furnishings of our ambiance is unacceptable: the new energy must be incorporated into a contemporary form.

[1925]

HANDIWORK

THE FILM ACTOR-MANNEQUIN is that person who is able to express any given assignment by the director with his entire body: his face, his hands, his trunk, his legs. For the actor-mannequin's work, the director gives him one or another expressive combinations, while the cinematographer expresses them most vividly in plastic form. Thus, work on each film scene should proceed organized systematically and harmonically.

In our former—pre-Revolutionary—cinema no one even thought about this. Now, not only are people thinking about it, they are trying to institute it into their work, their screen life, little by little.

Of course, hands and feet mostly attract the attention of actors and directors, preoccupying and interesting them above others, as these parts of the body, being the most expressive, characteristically emphasize both the type of the scenario and its psychological essence.

The development of this crucial question has been retarded here by our mass, national inability to govern the movement of our hands and feet in our own environment.

Observe yourself, observe your friends and acquaintances. On entering a room, we don't know what to do with our hands; we busy them with inexpressive and senseless activity. We sit with our legs crossed or in a heap, or with a hand draped over the back of a chair. The pockets of our trousers are always occupied by confused hands—if only so we don't lose them—or palms placed together, or hands folded across our chest or more comfortably situated somewhere behind our backs.

To stand on our feet with a proper distribution of weight of our bodies, to hold our hands at our sides, or to sit normally without our legs crossed or in a heap—this seems organically impossible for us.

The culture in which we had control of our bodies is lost—all body articulations are either undisciplined or unintentional, giving us away and not consciously controlled.

At the same time, we are aware that hands are capable of expressing literally everything: social origin, character, health, profession, the relationship of the individual to reality—with feet having much the same capability.

[1926]

WILL . . . TENACITY . . . EYE

OUR CINEMA is rich in opportunities and poor in qualified workers. We desire a great deal, but are not in a position to accomplish it: not for anyone.

That is why the emergence of a fine worker in the film should be extremely gratifying, especially in present conditions.

Our craft demands precise, responsible work, but, unfortunately, such elementary production demands on workers are seldom applied. World opinion and the artistic quality shown by capable people, capable *directors*, are far from being important. We have our own, our own *workers*, who comprehend contemporary life, who feel its rhythm and significance, and we have other people who, despite their working in the contemporary idiom, work along "antique" lines—as itinerants.

Such are the "bread-and-butter" directors, according to distribution officials, and few things are more invidious to film culture than their work. Everything done in fresh ways, everything done in the spirit of fulfilling given tasks, is the work of today; while every piece of hack-work, even though termed "artistic" by "critics" and costing hundreds of thousands of rubles, is the work of the past, bygone days.

That is why I am writing about Eisenstein-as-director, absolutely capable of evolving into the most significant fighter for a film culture, so indispensable to modern life.

The success of the films *Strike* and *The Battleship Potemkin* immediately gave the young director his well-deserved popularity as a

Soviet filmmaker. But one must not forget that his success was a somewhat costly one, and no criticism has been applied—neither in a single article, nor in a single analysis, professionally and substantially analytical of Eisenstein's work.

Almost everyone was ecstatic with joy, celebrated and unrestrainedly delighted in the new look of our cinematography; and it seems that the period of such acceptance of *Strike* and *The Battleship Potemkin* must be superseded by a serious analysis of their direction and some account of the future capabilities of the director.

Without claiming to make exhaustive appraisal of these films, one wants at least to attempt an accounting of those aspects that most characteristically and instantly strike the eye in watching them.

Let us begin with *Strike*—the first work and the first victory in our film and general press.

In this agit-film, for the first time and realistically, without operatic falseness, without pasted on mustaches and beards, without "Russian-style tea-towels," our actuality was portrayed, captured almost cinematographically, almost truthfully. After all that we had previously seen on the screen, this accomplishment astonished everyone.

It is worthwhile to recall any given film, even from among those shown today, to avaluate it seriously, for all the lies, all the operatically theatrical deformity of the "art" of our film directors to become apparent.

Eisenstein, as virtually the first person in agit-films, led people out of the props and trappings of the studio and showed things which had been well conceived but poorly constructed. Things and environments which were actual—factories, locomotives, cranes, industrial housing, etc.

Hardly any one of the other directors even thought of using the aforementioned materials, and this was Eisenstein's major victory in cinema.

He is more a director of the *shot*—tasteful and expressive—than of montage and human movement. Eisensteinian shots always overpower the rest; in the main, it is they that constitute the success of his works. It is enough simply to remember the hosing episode in *Strike*, the infinite savoring of these photogenic pieces of film, to become absolutely convinced of the director's fine "*eye*," of his particular love of the plastically expressive shot.

The montage of *Strike* is significantly weaker. It is overdone; it betrays a preoccupation with an unnecessarily rapid editing tempo, undeveloped into any system. Everything is simply too fragmented, there are unrelated aspects; but, principally, there is an absence of a single line of movement in the juxtaposition of images and of a single thematic line. For example, in the very weakest, the last part of the execution: the associative montage—the carnage and parallel butchery of the workers—is hardly a prerogative to transform the event into the form that resulted. This shot of the slaughter was not prepared to support a second line of action, incomplete as it is.

In *The Battleship Potemkin* an example of a correct application of association is the shot of the ship's doctor's pince-nez dangling from the rope. While it is true that the line of action here is a single one, in the case of parallel constructions, the same firm, logical connections must be observed in applying an association.

It is hardly worthwhile discussing the barrels—the habitation of the hooligans—and the eccentrically hanging cats, for after the theater, after *The Wise Man*, it is forgivable that a theatrical director be not completely cinematic, especially if the piece in question is one of the finest on our screens. *The Battleship Potemkin* is a film of indisputably great significance, of great weight, much more so than *Strike*. The main thing in this film is that it is *convincing* and that a complete entity, a whole, is captured on film by the director.

That is why it is captivating; even the colored flag, not reproducible on black-and-white film, is apprehended more and more not only as a symbol, but also because of the unexpectedness of the presence of coloring. Generally, it is not worthwhile to color frames, for it would not be very long before one would start to "brighten up" blood or the flame of a fire. It follows that the successes that this film has enjoyed in comparison with *Strike* ought to be traced.*

* A variant of *The Battleship Potemkin* contained hand-tinted sequences. R.L.

First of all, it is vital to ascertain the raising of the quality of montage. Ranking with bad montage, is the end of the first part—the sailor, washing the plate, turns it not in accordance with the movement of his head—and such places; but there is such a convincing montage sequence as the bombing of the Odessa Theater with the startled lions. Theatricality—in the hanging cats and the barrels of *Strike*. No, when it comes to the movement of crowds and actors, it ought to be better and more integral. In fact, in his future work Eisenstein certainly ought to apply himself to the actor's element and to mass scenes, as they are not always *structured*, and if they are structured, then not always grammatically. This, then, is the rudimentary aspect, in terms of the technical element, that ought to be analyzed in the evaluation of the work of Eisenstein.

The basis of his success in art, the basis that elicits a particular respect, is his will in production—an emphasis on and the ability to select significant, self-serving themes.

Others could not do better.

In a short period of time Eisenstein has successfully grown into a master, has grown well, since apart from talent, he is possessed of *will*, *tenacity*, and a *sharp eye*.

[1926]

WHY I AM NOT WORKING

I AM endlessly pelted with questions concerning the reasons why I am not given work as a film director. Finally, I decided to use this invitation from the editors of *Kino** to give a complete explanation of what is happening with me in production and how I regard all of this.

This pause has been sixteen months long, and it began after I completed *The Death Ray*—a film that is, for me, an attempt to affirm a genuine technique and mastery in Soviet cinema.

In general, I consider it crucial to be aware in our craft of what a person wishes and what he can do.

I take into account the impossibility of successes in production without the use of a single, organized, and cohesive group.

That is why I prefer in the future to develop my work along the lines of accomplishing the maximal mastery of film within the context of developing the collective which I have headed.

The themes of the scenarios, which have served as the material for the production experiences developed in *Mr. West* and *The Death Ray*, are unquestionably inadequate, but the ideological slander that was raised after the release of the last film is utterly undeserved.

It must not be forgotten that up to now all the accomplishments of our group should be evaluated only as a bill of fare of Soviet film technique—the skills of our craft—and not as finished films. At one

* A weekly newspaper of the Soviet film industry.

time, the public, the critics, and the studios were forewarned of this. It was imperative for me to give the filmed "bills of fare" the kind of form that would insure their financial solvency, which, in fact, we were lucky enough to have done.

In order to show what was most important in these films, a clever theme was unnecessary; what was needed was enough Americanism to prove the high level of our technical skill (in organized hands), comparable with the most technically skilled Americans.

One must regret that the demand for fine workers in Soviet cinema is still insufficiently developed.

But this is all right; this stems from an unfamiliarity and deepest ignorance of the business, and with time it will pass; that is why none of the knowledgeable craftsmen need feel hurt by the critics who, while they condemn *The Death Ray* for its ideology, overlooked my task and the form in which it could have been realized.

I promised to prove that despite our poor technical resources we *could* produce an inexpensive film of a European-style virtuosity, and *I have fulfilled my promise.*

But the conditions for the fulfillment of this task were so burdensome that the thematic side of the work might very well have been unsatisfactory—this was my inalienable right as a human being, in attempting to solve a major, important, but as yet unresolved problem.

After *Ray* it was vital to demonstrate one's work on psychological, deeply dramatic film works.

The low cost of production, the convincing internal work of the actor-mannequin—these are the very problems that deserve to be broadened now.

From this moment on begins that struggle with administrators and producers of film enterprises, which still prevents me from even attempting to produce dramatic chamber-films.

The habit of the obstinacy of workers has, apparently, frightened the film studios, and in order to insure Kuleshov against an obsession with "Americanism," he is being offered the most venerable, the most theatrical, and therefore the most worthless, film actors and staff.

In despair and poverty, my film group was formed and developed over a period of five hungry years—it grew and matured and *has a right to work.*

The very formation of this group was not impelled by whimsy but has been dictated by the impossibility of resolving new problems with personnel unprepared for their resolution and the corresponding work. That is the reason that I will be unable to do a single new piece of work without my collective of actor-mannequins and assistants, and without the prerogative to select those from among them who are best suited to my needs as a director.

Otherwise, all that has been planned will be unfulfilled—neither I nor the cinema needs this.

The suspension of the established method of conquering film technique will lead to hack-work—why do we need that when there is so much of it as it is?

Only with a loss of reason or in dishonesty will I agree to work without the right to work alongside all the members of our collective and in accordance with our fair details.

It cannot be otherwise, and, indeed, I have not the right to do otherwise.

[1926]

DAVID GRIFFITH AND CHARLIE CHAPLIN

TWO WORLD MASTERS laid the foundations of the school of cinematography—David Griffith and Charlie Chaplin.

Griffith worked both in pure cinematography and on the histrionics of his actors, bringing them to communicate their psychological states by means of the most complex movements of their mechanisms.

However, these movements were not merely elementary grimaces but were reflexological and precisely worked out, which is why they fulfill their desired purpose. In the case of Griffith, actors did not simply bulge-out their eyes, say, at some horror, but performed other movements more accurately communicating their state of being.

The biting of lips, rumination, the twining of the hands, the touching of objects, and so on, are the characteristic signs of the Griffith performance. It is not difficult to realize that these came close to the moments of actual extreme suffering and, most often, to those moments approaching hysteria.

An entire film cannot be constructed entirely of strong emotions, which is why Griffith filled the interim spaces between scenes of heavy suffering with pure cinedynamics.

Constructing his films in this way he achieved extraordinary results, and for a long time neither his work nor his scenarios were bested.

It was Chaplin who overstepped the classical scenario with his *A Woman of Paris.* In terms of its construction this scenario may be termed ideal, and it demonstrated a new method of film work. Chaplin virtually obliterated the elementary portrayal of emotion communicated facially. He demonstrated the deportment of a person in various aspects of his life by means of his relationship to things, to objects. Relative to the state of things, the method of the treatment of the hero vis-à-vis his environment and people around him changes, as does his conduct.

Thus, all work can be reduced to the establishment of various labor processes, since something is done with objects: violating or ordering their commonplace organization, handling them either rationally or irrationally, the actor-mannequin acts out the processes of labor. The labor process—its mechanics; then, movement; then the ultimate material of the cinema. Thus, the work of the scenarist must come down to the expression of a fable through the organization of people interacting with objects, facilitated by the behavior of the person and his reflexes. *A Woman of Paris* demonstrated that these are indisputably filmic, and can be interesting elements of movement.

Many say that *A Woman of Paris* turned out well not because the scenario was good: "We would have never related the scenario to the production." An absolute answer: it is precisely the scenario of *A Woman of Paris* which is exceptionally good.

In it one thing follows another in an uninterrupted logical connection: not one single episode can be discarded—else the uninterrupted cinedramaturgical significance is lost.

When we seek to imitate the Chaplinesque scenario here, an intolerable succession of episodes is tossed in of people with objects, such that any one can be either eliminated or replaced. The extraordinary quality of the scenario of *A Woman of Paris* lies in the fact that nothing can be eliminated in it, since each episode is indispensable and mandatory. If the scenario of *A Woman of Paris* were given to a bad director, it would undoubtedly still turn out well; in Chaplin's hands it was genius.

[1928]

THE REHEARSAL METHOD

CAN ONE continue with the existing forms of the method of rehearsal? Certainly one cannot, and before all else, because of the technique of rehearsal. For today, there is a host of defects, if for no other reason than that we rehearse not a film, but only the actor's performance, not only that, but we rehearse it quite primitively—always from a single point of view. Working in this way, without adequate qualifications or with weakened attention, we can fall into a certain theatricalism in the construction of the *mise en scène*. Therefore, the work in the area of rehearsal method now must be improved, developed. Opportunities to rehearse must be increased, to bring this work closer to the cinema. What is fundamental, what must be categorically taken up, is the construction of the scene. In *The Great Consoler* we used a scene "in the style of the year 1920," conceived in the State School of Cinematography. It is of course evident that this rough, primitive scene would be unsatisfactory today. Other constructions could be used, for instance, the connection of scenes disposed in two series; the montage for this, and likewise the rearrangement of objects and props, would be made much easier. For rehearsal it is necessary to create not one scene, but two at a time, performed before combinations of backgrounds already used, or perhaps, it would be better to set the scene so that the curtains would be divided the full width of both scenes.

The basic defect in the rehearsal method in the conditions of the aforementioned scene is that the director establishes the point of view, all the time running all around the performing actors, that is, grabbing the cameraman under his arms, running with him to the right—one camera angle; to the left—a second angle; to the rear—a third, and so on. In the final analysis the director will have to check his scenes from one point of view—from his own director's chair.

How can we circumvent this defect of the abovementioned stage?

One must apply what has been applied in the theater when a quick set change is required—a rotating disc on the floor. But a rotating disc must be used for the actor's performance, not for the imagination of the scenery. The performing actors should turn with this disc during the action, so that the action would *not be seen from a single point of view.* This is the most crucial thing to achieve in the studios when the rehearsal areas are being equipped. Then, it is necessary to think through the system of lighting. Perhaps, it is possible to set the lights according to the principle of the projected light (focused beams, auto headlights, etc.), to separate by lighting the "long" shots from the "medium" shots. This will make easier a montage perception of the rehearsal.

The construction of a convenient rehearsal stage is the technical task of the coming days.

Along the lines of the sample rehearsal stage cited, we are conducting our work together with S. M. Eisenstein. On Potylikha Street, the new building for GIK is being built,* and we have offered to build a special *experimental rehearsal film-theater* there, which can be used for demonstration not only to our Union, but also for international audiences. This will not be an ordinary theater. This construction, which we are describing, is interesting not only for cinematography but also for the theater in general. Together with S. M. Eisenstein and the GIK architects we established the fundamental principle for the construction of this theater. We have three stages: a central one and two side ones. (See Fig. 1.) In the center of the theater

* Plans changed. Instead of being built alongside Mosfilm, the film school was built next to the Gorky Studio, on the other side of Moscow. R.L.

auditorium, there is a large rotating disc on which seats for spectators are distributed. When necessary, the spectator on this disc rotates either to the right or left side stage; that is, we will be able by montage to rotate the viewer to face either the one stage, the other, or the third.

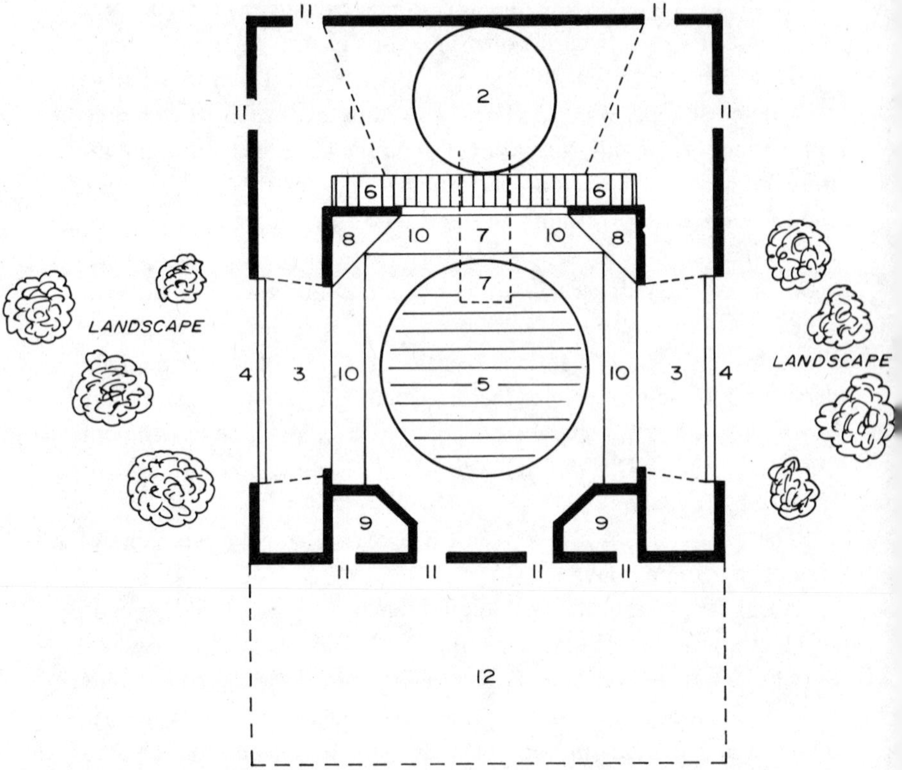

FIGURE 1. An approximate design for a film rehearsal theater, proposed by Sergei Eisenstein and Lev Kuleshov.

1. Main stage. 2. Disc for scene changes. 3. Two side stages. 4. Sliding doors opening onto landscape. 5. Central rotating disc with seats for spectators. 6. Moving sidewalk for main stage. 7. Portable minibridge for "long shots." 8. Two screens for projection. 9. Two projection booths. 10. Orchestra space. 11. Doors (also serving the audience). 12. Theater foyer. A director's booth can be located on the central disc. Apart from the three stages the action can also take place on the central disc, when the chairs for the audience are moved onto the stage (1).

There is a rotating disc in the central stage itself for *the rotation of the action.*

All three stages are connected each to the other and to the actors; it is possible to cross from one stage to another.

The large stages are not very deep, but they must have back walls, which slide apart giving onto the landscape, and the viewer can see between these stages, a forest to one side, a field to the other.

The side stages which give onto the landscape beyond (see Fig. 1) are convenient in that massive scenes may be rehearsed, if needed, with passing cavalry, artillery, tractors, automobiles, and so on (this of course is for "great spectaculars").

Between the stages two screens are located. Over the spectators' seats or by the entrance into the theater, a control booth is situated, from which signals are given for the operation of the curtains (each stage must have two or three curtains), for the operation of the lights, and so on.

On the main stage, in keeping with the system of the Japanese theater, a little bridge is proposed, which can be moved into the spectators' hall, so that a "close-up" of the actor may be shown. The Japanese show what are virtually cinematic "close-ups" in their theater. When a very minute performance must be shown on the face of an actor, he goes onto that bridge. We can achieve this principally by means of the isolation of lighting: the actor steps out before the spectator upstage and performs the most subtle work, say, with his eyelashes or lips. Then in an instant, the lights are extinguished, and the bridge is removed in darkness.

In addition, we propose to construct a moving sidewalk at the proscenium of the central stage (of the conveyer-belt type) which can move in either direction, in order to depict a man running in place, or to pan with the action.

The project is also interesting in that, when needed, the chairs may be removed from the basic disc in the center of the hall, moved to the stage, and then the actors can proceed in the center of the theater, on the central rotating disc. Of course, the project can be simplified in construction. The central rotating disc need not be constructed, but a rotating armchair of the "American" variety may be substituted, which will allow the viewer himself to alter his position and to see either one stage or another. It is possible to construct it so that only one side stage opens onto "nature" (an exterior set) or so that both open, and so on.

I do not know whether the entire project can be realized in the Moscow GIK (Government Institute of Kino), whether it appears possible for the project to be built to completion, whether, unfortunately, it will only be possible to build it only on the second floor, and then probably with only the side stages opening onto "nature."

What is extremely important in the completion of this project is that, though at first glance it appears complex in its architectural construction, in actuality it is simple because all that exists in the interior of the theatrical hall is not related to its architectural completion, but only to its *proper equipment*. Architecturally, one need only construct a square—a room with two doors that open onto nature—while the stages, the scaffolding, the discs, and so on, would be only the equipment of this room.

This theater is a perfect rehearsal hall, with a definite development of the rehearsal scene "modeled after 1920," in which *The Great Consoler* was rehearsed.

The theater will permit us to improve maximally the technique of rehearsal.

How then must further work proceed along the lines of the organizational development of the rehearsal method?

At the last plenary session of the Central Committee of the Union [of Art Workers] there were a great many speeches, and, in particular, the speech by V. I. Pudovkin, dealing with Soviet film direction. The commonly held opinion was that there are many directors, no matter how freshly inexperienced they may be, who want to be "no worse then Eisenstein, Dovzhenko and their like," immediately, no matter what; that is, whatever is not attributable to the director, is invariably "in an artistic direction." Because each director in his first film, whatever else happens, wants to "rub noses with Pudovkin and Eisenstein," the organization of our cinema does not have its own creative face, as we can detect this, say, in most theaters. When we are told about the Moscow Art Theater, we can visualize a definite artistic direction; when the Kamernyi Theater is discussed, we know how it differs from the Moscow Art Theater; when the Meyerhold Theater is discussed, we again imagine a new distinct physiognomy for this theater.

But when a new film studio is named, we can seldom, if ever, visualize its creative face, since it produces films of any style, any character, and often films that are simply "undistinguishable." To be sure, the cinema serves a broad audience, it shows its products to a multi-millioned mass, while the theater is limited in its scale and its material. Therefore a complete analogy between the theater and cinema cannot be made, but to some extent every film organization, like the theater, must have a definite creative face, even if due to the *leading directors*—more complicated than in the theater, but a distinct face nonetheless.

This will possibly happen only when future directors are responsible not only for themselves but *for a whole group of young directors* who will be working with them, with whom a given director in charge might be in a production and creative capacity. Even in the Kamerny Theater it is not only Tairov who directs, there are others; in the Meyerhold Theater it is not only Meyerhold; in the Moscow Art Theater it is not only Stanislavsky. Working under the leading director, other directors develop. Moreover, it is clear that young directors will outstrip the directors in charge, when mature, and will become independent, major creative individuals, and in their turn, will gather around themselves new young directors, and so on.

Here is the plan of operation that would be absolutely correct and normal for the future years. The entire question is how to approach this plan. If this plan is realized, the quality of production of all directors will rise unquestionably.

The rehearsal method has made a beginning for the realization of this work plan.

The transition stage to it is the work of a single qualified director over two parallel productions. This can be implemented in 1934, but by 1935 it will already be possible to surpass it with a grouping of several directors around a head director (say, four or five parallel productions).

I shall try to explain how it is possible to begin implementing two parallel productions by one director.

What do we have as a result of the rehearsal method? The main thing we have is the planned adjustment of organized work of the *entire* group. Before the rehearsal method, this did not exist. Now we have a genuine, actual organization of the *period of preparation.* It can be said that a period of preparation was wanting prior to the rehearsal method. The rehearsal method obliterates bustle, yelling, hysteria at the studio. We know that the majority of our film studios is characterized by unrelieved screaming, running, and panic. The rehearsal method at its best liquidates this fussing, trouble, and "mix-ups." The work is built by plan and organization. With the rehearsal method completely new, hitherto unknown forms of responsibility emerge. Previously one could never find the guilty party in "mix-ups." A poor picture or bad set decorations would come out, poor rushes would come out—in the conditions existing in almost every studio it is impossible to find the actually guilty person: each will put the blame on the other.

The rehearsal method completely, exactly, and precisely distributes the functions of each worker, and that is why the opportunity *to ask* emerged, the opportunity to be responsible for one's part of the job, the opportunity for precise and daily checking of work completion, while earlier the checking of work completion in film production was chaotic. That is why the director, during this form of rehearsal, can determine, as never before, the profile of production work of his production unit, his nearest co-workers.

And to the extent that a director knows the production profile of his unit, he knows what each person can do best. This produces the possibility to exploit maximally each member of the unit. If one or another person was not used fully in production in the pre-rehearsal method and worked only adequately, then in the rehearsal method he works maximally. We know that ordinarily a creative worker at the studio (a director, an assistant director, a cameraman) expends the major portion of his energy on not what is directly assigned. One to two hours each day are spent on creative work, while all the rest of the time is spent in rushing about, or "cussing," searching for objects, or overcoming the organizational machine's problems.

Now, with the application of the rehearsal method, the director and his assistants have creative time (which, previously, was spent in surmounting problems in the organizational machine) freed, and it can be completely spent on creative efforts.

What must the studio manager do, if he is told all of this? He must not begin to reason along the lines of least resistance. He must not say: "Ivanov has some free time, let's give him something else to do." This is only half-right, but it is not enough to load someone with work; one must do so reasonably. The remaining time must be spent in the broadening of creative work, not in technical production work. Excess time must be filled creatively. How should it be filled? It is extremely easy to fill it—not to throw this time away. Since the collective exists, the members of which are tied to each other, it is important not to work off "free" time on some sort of other film of another director, but to utilize it on the work of the second parallel picture, with the same director. In the case of free time, two parallel films ought to be planned, since a director can turn his functions over to his assistants. During the shooting of *The Great Consoler*, my work was so structured: whenever there were complex scenes for the sound man, I assigned this work to the sound man; for the silent camera operator, to the silent camera operator; for the actors, I assigned the work to the assistant. I could assign the shooting—because during the rehearsal everyone knew everything well, when and how everything should be done—while my presence during the shooting was unnecessary. Precisely in this way I can exploit this opportunity for two films with one director and one unit. There are cases when the unit of a single film can be extremely unwieldy; for instance, during the shooting of the film *Deserter*, the unit comprised twenty-two people.

I propose the following composition of a group in two parallel productions:

The head director, the assistant director (speaking of the assistant, perhaps one is not enough, two are needed—that would be more appropriate), one very good creative advisor to the director, a sound recordist and his two assistants.

The entire system of work is founded on the proper use of assistants. The assistants are qualified people, for the most part graduates of the Film Institute, whose qualifications are sufficient but who are lacking practice. Under the tutelage of the "head", an assistant can produce superb results.

This utilization of assistants in the rehearsal method is marvelous, and it permits the simultaneous shooting of two films.

In addition, a silent cameraman is included in the unit, with two assistants, one set designer for both pictures, a head costumer, a make-up man, the chief lighting man (we have now introduced chief lighting man into groups at Mezhrabpom, which is extremely convenient). Perhaps one can do without the cinematographer, with his two assistants, *and* a silent cameraman, in addition to which there are two to three technical advisors and a manager.

As it is, this becomes a group of some 17 to 19 persons, which is fewer than the group on one film, *Deserter*, where there were 22 people.

Let us calculate how many are needed for one average film, if we shoot by the parallel method.

A group of 14 persons is needed for one film, though in fact this is the most modest group (when we were shooting *The Great Consoler* we had a group of 14 by the end of the film). Thus, during the shooting of a very modest film such as *The Great Consoler*, a group of 14 is needed, while with my suggested system, we can do with 19 people for two films. This will create a great economy since to do two separate films, 19 people would be needed for each film; double that and you have 38.

How will production go on with two films? It will go on simply: joint treatments, direction, and supervision on the part of the director, and differentiated assignments. Differentiated assignments will facilitate the making of both films with unconditionally high quality. The work should be conducted by means of a system of assistants, as I conducted it in the shooting of the film, *The Great Consoler.* When I left, having checked over the scene, the assistant would develop it. I put together the shot list, handed it over to the cameraman and he would shoot it with his assistants. I would arrive at the shooting session, check over the general work situation and could leave—the shooting went on without me. Both the cameramen (sound and silent) can confidently turn over this work to their assistants.

Thus, this method permits the shooting of two films, without reducing their quality, if the director's and chief cameramen's leadership is good. To touch on the question of production time, then, if we take the production of a film at 100 percent, we will have not 200, but 175–180 percent of the production time—using the method of parallel shooting of two films—which means that the value of the two films will add up to 175–180 percent instead of 200 normally assigned. Why? Because we have once again a fundamental advantage that derives precisely from the parallel shooting of two films: we have the opportunity actually to plan, and account for, a production.

The rehearsal method brings us nearer to some kind of socialistic form of a film production process. To work socialistically—this means, first and foremost, to take a concrete account of something and to plan it; and the rehearsal method with the simultaneous production of two films provides the opportunity maximally to produce an accounting of, and maximally to distribute the work and personnel into, two films at once, and likewise the very production of these films. While the sets for one film are being constructed, we are able to shoot the other film in the second studio. We are able at last to work along simultaneous lines or along lines of parallel work (one assistant prepares one scene for one film, the other, for the other film; one works the first shift, the other the second. All of this can be accounted for and planned. This allows a saving of time and money with the preservation of quality).

Accordingly, the development of the rehearsal period must occur in the following manner: in the beginning, two parallel productions of one director, and then the creative consolidation of directors in charge with young directors. That is how a creative collective is comprised of a group of directors, each with his own production plan.

Now we pass to the relationship of the rehearsal method to the instructional work of film institutes.

First of all, the rehearsal method provides the opportunity to construct work much more integrally and rationally with the qualifying courses at GIK.

The basic flaw of the Kiev and Moscow state film institutes is that the instructor-directors appear in the institutes "on the go," * limited by episodic lectures, and without showing students the actual practice of directorial work.

It seems to me that the more correct form of work for head directors of film institutes is the staging in rehearsals of excerpts from literary works or the staging of film scenarios by the institute's students themselves on the specially equipped stage.

Agreements must be reached, it seems to me, with master-instructors as to separate rehearsal productions of students under the supervision of their instructors. This will spare students from listening to merely episodic lectures and will ensure the consistent leadership of directors. Additionally, such an approach, on the one hand, will improve and develop the rehearsal method in the cinema, while, on the other hand, it will familiarize students with this method of work also in production. Secondly, the rehearsal method will provide students of GIK the opportunity to submit the work for their degree realistically and responsibly. To this day, final degree productions have not been completed, and if they have been, then very primitively, in the guise of some sort of étude, the briefest excerpt, and so on.

The rehearsal method provides an opportunity to produce solid responsible degree works—project films with director's scenarios and the rehearsal of entire performances of actors.

When an engineer completes his university studies, he does his

* Directors who held teaching posts at film institutes often carried on sporadic teaching duties while in production. R.L..

degree work, let us say, on a project for a railroad bridge or a project for a factory.

Likewise a young filmmaker-director graduates from the Institute to a production project. This production project is the scenario worked out directorially, the director's explication, the photography of actors and make-up, the set designs and costumes, and most importantly, the performance of a rehearsal of the coming production. With this kind of degree work it becomes possible to judge the actual knowledge and abilities of the young director. (The opportunity for demonstrating separate scenes of the project already shot and cut is not excluded; but the rehearsal performance—this is nonetheless basic to the degree work.)

In conclusion one has to discuss the forms of instruction at GIK in connection with the rehearsal work of instructors both in actual production and in the classroom.

Now, as never before, is the chance for GIK to turn its face toward production, and for production, likewise, to turn its face toward GIK.

At GIK, the instruction will be (in the final director's course) concerned with the rehearsal method. Some scenarios will be staged. Actors will have to participate in the performed rehearsal. There will not be enough actors in the acting course at GIK for this.

Where should the remaining actors be found for this?

They will have to be invited from production, from the production units of the instructor-directors. For their part, student-directors and student-actors must visit the work of their instructor-director, to observe it, and to participate actively in it. We know that staff actors of a given studio have lots of free time; instead of passing that time strolling about, it will be used beneficially and educationally in the rehearsal work at GIK.

Both directors and cameramen, and other members of the production unit, vitally need to do a production experiment from time to time. They can do it in rehearsal at GIK, while students only benefit from this in terms of their education.

Thus, in mutual cooperation, in the amalgamating of GIK institutional and professional production work, based on the rehearsal method, young specialists are forged, who are closely bound to production work.

It seems to me that from this essay clear, broad perspectives and possibilities for the rehearsal method ought to follow, both for production and pedagogy.

[1934]

OUR FIRST EXPERIENCES

BEFORE THE REVOLUTION I was working as an artist with the A. Khanzhonkov Company. I made one film there—this was the first Russian film made according to American montage. It was called *Engineer Prite's Project.* Then I went to work with Kozlovsky, Yurev and Co., where I made a film with V. Polonsky (*The Unfinished Love Song*). This film was not particularly noteworthy; I made it simply to survive, for money. The titles for the film were written in verse by the writer, Smolny. (They were dreadful.)

The Revolution began. For the most part, during these first years of the Revolution, I worked on the battlefronts; in charge of the filming of the campaigns of the Red Army with various cameramen. Cameramen such as Tisse, Lemberg, Yermolov, and others, worked with me. My principal student was Eduard Tisse, who demonstrated miraculous documentary skills. For example, he and I shot the advance of Kolchak. We were riding together in an open car into the attack of the Red armored cars, and got stuck, accidentally finding ourselves some fifty paces from a Cossack cannon. The Cossacks started firing at us point-blank with their artillery. And Tisse somehow continued to film every single one of the discharging explosions directed at him. He filmed them hand-holding the Debrie, a heavy camera.

It was extremely interesting to apply the practice of close-up montage to documentary film. At this time, none of the cameramen had the slightest idea that a documentary could be constructed the same way as a dramatic film—with close-ups, using montage; that it was possible to shoot from "high angles," "low angles," that it was unnecessary to shoot with crisp detail in relief, clearly and expressively.

Cameramen considered such filming utterly inadmissible and ungrammatical.

What is interesting is that this very Tisse, who is now working with a world famous personality, in no way wanted to work with montage. And, while one of Tisse's specializations now is that he shoots with a variety of angles with virtuosity, varied points of view in montage, earlier, it had been necessary to argue with him endlessly, to swear at him, almost to come to blows. We were prepared to "fight to the death" to prove ourselves right. But I was so certain of the rightness of montage that I prevailed.

The same arguments took place also with A. Lemberg. After they saw what was shot on the screen in a viewable and edited state, these selfsame cameramen immediately became enthusiasts of close-ups, and montage, and the organized shooting of documentaries. At this very time, Dziga Vertov was developing as a unit manager, and became extremely interested in the new methods of montage filming. Gradually, he evolved from a technical organizer of work into an artistic one—into a documentary director. He studied montage close-ups and the organized structure of the shot scrupulously.

I shall introduce another interesting biographical fact. It was in the Urals. The cameraman and I were returning from the front. In Sverdlovsk (formrly Yekatirinburg), I met a young boy, a Red Army soldier, Leonid Obolensky, with whom I became acquainted. We began to talk about film. I explained to him my point of view, my theories, concerning the cinema, and we became interested in each other. Obolensky had been discharged from the army, and I gave him a letter to the newly inaugurated film school in Moscow. The letter was addressed to V. P. Gardin, who was the head and representative of the school. When I returned from the front, I found Obolensky already a student of this school. The instructors of this school were qualified, but from my viewpoint, "of a conservative inclination." They worked only on histrionics and purely theatrical conventions (with the exception of V. Gardin, who was "more left"). They had no knowledge of specifically filmic technique and felt that it was virtually useless. At the examinations, on which I happened to chance, one group of students were "flunked" as totally talentless. One of the failing female students was Chekulayeva. She is presently an actress at Mezhrabpomfilm. At that particular time I began to prepare an étude for reexamination with extreme precision, concentrating on each movement (I did not have a theory of acting then). T. Chekulayeva is an extraordinarily gifted actress, and the étude came out very well. What is more, I proceeded intuitively from the beginning in this étude, without theoretical analysis; I applied the method of a maximally precise structure of movement, step by step, detail by detail. When Chekulayeva went for her reexamination the board of examiners was surprised and astonished, as this was the best étude ever performed at the school. Then I immediately took on the entire party of failed students and, within a few days (they happened to be the most talented in the school), they received the best marks in the reexamination.

At that time I found out that two students had done a parody on that excerpt which I had staged for those being reexamined. I was shown this parody. It was really extraordinarily funny and wonderfully precisely and deftly made. It was made by students A. Raikh and A. Khokhlova.

True, Khokhlova said, after a few years, they had tried to do these excerpts seriously, not intending a parody. But at that time, while everyone was laughing, they insisted that that was exactly how they were working.

Soon I was invited to be an instructor at the State Film School (GTK), given a workshop—a separate class—and of course all those students whom I had then helped with their examination, signed into my class.

But at this point I was needed for filming on the Western Polish front. A member of the Revolutionary War Soviet of the Western front, Comrade Smilga, offered to base a film unit on his train. At that time, I, the cameraman, N. V. Yermolov, and my students from the film school—Khokhlova, Obolensky, and Raikh—traveled to the front and did a semi-documentary, semi-fiction wartime film, based on the material of the Polish War. We created a very simple scenario and shot the film—half-acted, half-documentary. This was the first Soviet film based on the material of the Civil War. It was in the year 1920. It was told to me later, and I'm not certain how accurate it is, that V. I. Lenin liked the film a great deal and apparently he saw it twice and praised it. We cut the film, of course, on the principle of montage and working very precisely with the actors (at that time we regarded them as actor-mannequins). This was the first piece of work in the new method, made by the students of the film school.

Having returned from the front, we continued our work at the State Film School and here approached the establishment of the artistic bases of the training of film actors thoroughly and began to work out the practicum of this training. Podobed and Komarov, who now (1934) work at Mezhrabpomfilm, also studied in my class. At that time we were developing the theory of the axes (of human movement) and the metric web.

Having trained for some time, we completed a number of educational études already in the form of complete playlets with montage scene changes. A performance night was planned at the school, which later became a series of formal performances. Four pieces were presented. The first piece was titled "At No. 147 St. Joseph's Street" (a reminder that the year was 1921). The essence of this piece was that some sort of dancer had returned home after a performance and lay down to sleep. Complete darkness set in. A flashlight, which would perform various lighting manipulations, appeared in the room. It became apparent that the dancer had been kidnapped, then taken to an unfamiliar street, St. Joseph's, No. 147. There she was tied to a table and raped. In the course of the rape, a fight ensued, and the dancer got free. This was the first theme.

The second was more complex, constructed on twenty-four scene changes, continuously following one another. The performance of the étude continued for thirty to forty minutes. It was called "The Venetian Stocking" (scenario by V. Turkin).

I have forgotten to point out that in the first étude, in "No. 147 St. Joseph's Street," there was a student named A. Chistyakov, who was already some forty years old, and was working in cinema at this school (prior to school he had been an accountant). Besides him, Khokhlova, Pudovkin, and Raikh worked on this étude.

Khokhlova, Podobed, and Pudovkin also worked on "The Venetian Stocking," along with several other comrades, who filled minor roles (in that latter category, Raikh, then Inkizhinov). The contents of "The Stocking" were roughly as follows: A doctor receives a female patient. The doctor's wife (Khokhlova) is extremely jealous. She confronts the doctor (Podobed) in an hysterical fit, and this fit goes on for about 150 meters, worked out in the most complex, semi-acrobatic series of movements. Then the doctor, distressed, leaves the house. He pauses in front of a velvet column, representing a street kiosk (pillar covered with placards and notices), reads and does not notice that a second person is walking around the other side of this pillar, duplicating his movements. They then see each other, and it happens that this person is his friend (Pudovkin). Podobed approaches the friend, and the friend gives him a lace, Venetian stocking, which dandies reputedly tie around their necks instead of neckties. (The play began with Pudovkin—the doctor's friend—tying this stocking around his own neck.)

Returning home, the doctor is reconciled with his wife and accidentally takes the stocking out of his pocket. A new hysterical fit results, which reaches its peak by means of a host of acrobatic exercises and grotesque constructions. At the end of these hysterics, the wife (Khokhlova) locks Podobed in the room. She leaves, while he escapes out of a window. She wanders along the streets, becomes hungry, and enters a restaurant. In this restaurant, Raikh magnificently depicts an orchestra. Pudovkin has been sitting in the restaurant. It appears that in the process of all the weeping, Khokhlova forgot her money. Then Pudovkin gallantly offers to pay for her. She reddens, becomes embarrassed, and leaves. (Apropos, I made a hat for Khokhlova, which probably weighed five kilos and was assembled from metal film cans used for reels—an architecturally sculptural construction. This was most characteristic of "the art of 1921".) On the street, Pudovkin catches up to Khokhlova. She has nowhere else to go, so she goes toward him. No sooner does he begin to woo her, while she grotesquely reacts in fear, then Podobed arrives. Then Pudovkin hides Khokhlova behind a screen. Podobed tells his friend that his wife doesn't give him any peace what with the other's stocking—she's jealous. Podobed leaves. Pudovkin pushes Khokhlova, tries to kiss her; she gives him a slap, while the latter performs a "back flip." Khokhlova returns home and begins to make it up with her husband. I don't remember exactly what happens next, but, in short, Pudovkin comes to visit, she is "stunned" from the surprise of seeing the chance acquaintance, and all is resolved to everyone's satisfaction and mutual benefit.

There was yet a third étude which was shorter—"The Apple." In this one, Komarov, Khokhlova, and Kravchenko worked together.

The fourth étude was called "The Ring"—a completely grotesque piece. Fogel worked in this one for the first time. And there was still another étude, which differed principally from the others I have described. This étude was the predecessor of my film, *By the Law.*

Everything we performed was very interesting and enjoyed great success, but was constructed grotesquely. These were comic pieces, and, more than that, they became comic not only because of the theme or subject, but also because of the exaggerated construction of movement. We wanted desperately to evolve into actual, real work. The étude, "Gold," became the first piece, planned along actual, real lines, but along very precise and clearly designed movements. This was the first cinematographic piece.

As in *By the Law*, the material for this étude was adapted by me from one of the stories of Jack London, "A Piece of Meat." But it was completely rewritten. It is interesting to note that when I began to stage "Gold," absolutely nothing would come out right for me the first few days. And we strove to stage the étude by traditional acting methods (internal emotion).

Since nothing would go right, one fine day I got angry and began to block literally each movement, each centimeter of the actors' movements, while the actors, already sufficiently experienced, at this time immediately related these schemes with actual emotion. In the sense of emotional and technical aspects, this work was considered very integrated, with emotion and technique going hand in hand.

The contents of "Gold" were as follows: A curtain rises, screens and cubes stand on stage. From various ends of the stage, from behind these very cubes and screens, people start running in several directions. They have been stealing something. The following episode was in a pharmacy. Pudovkin enters, playing a bandit, and talks the pharmacist into selling him some strychnine. The pharmacist sells it to him. While Pudovkin is in the pharmacy, Khokhlova and Podobed (two other crooks) come back home, unwrap a packet (this was an ordinary bookkeeping book, wrapped in a black, silk kerchief), opening it very slowly. The accounting book looked like a gold bar. The glitter of gold is reflected on Khokhlova and Podobed's faces. The gold "bewitches" them. Each of them begins to dream his own dreams, and then unexpectedly their glances meet, somewhat guarded, suspicious of each other. This was extremely well done by the author. Acted brilliantly by Khokhlova and Podobed, such a non-filmic, non-external work—a dream about what will happen with this gold, "how we'll live together later"—was absolutely impeccable. Podobed offers Khokhlova to kill Pudovkin with a knife, as he is soon to return. Pudovkin comes back, very happy, begins to brew some tea, pours it, adds the strychnine to all the glasses except his own, and talks his "friends" into drinking it. Podobed drinks the tea, Khokhlova sticks the knife into Pudovkin's back (by the way, when Pudovkin had come in, Podobed melancholically stood sharpening a razor).

The entire tea-drinking scene was staged on the principle that Khokhlova opens and shuts a desk drawer, so as to remove the knife unnoticed by Pudovkin. The play was centered on this drawer-pulling in and out for a long time. Pudovkin, stabbed by Khokhlova, fell complicatedly from the tabletop. This was a memorable "fall" by

Pudovkin (in the technical sense), one of which he remains proud to this day. While Pudovkin is falling, Podobed takes out a pistol and shoots Khokhlova. Then the dying Pudovkin beckons to Podobed with a finger and speaks into his ear: ". . . strychnine in the stomach." Podobed runs over to his glass, smells it and, in ten minutes, dies. He starts to have convulsions. When all three are completely inert, transformed into cold corpses, the étude finishes. Despite the extreme stylization of the scenario construction, this étude was done very realistically and filmically from the standpoint of the actors' performances.

All these pieces were combined into a public presentation. At first, we performed this program as a summary report, but then we received such a lot of requests for its presentation, that we preformed it continuously for some months. The school was, by then, I believe, a government technical institute. Effectively, all theatrical directors, film directors, producrs, and distributors (they still existed then) were coming to these performances. These spectacles were big news from the standpoint of actor performances and the structure of movement, and likewise the structure of the études themselves. People came to us even to study from these pieces.

Why did we create these spectacles and études?

Because we simply couldn't do anything else. There was no film stock then. The film, *On the Red Front*, was shot on positive stock, and was printed on primitive Russian film. There was a man called Minervin, who manufactured primitive positive (reversal) film stock. In his office the ink had been poured into shot glasses. He had a most interesting laboratory. For instance, he dried segments of already printed pieces (footage) on trees in his yard. He worked on Gorky Street; the yard was not very large. One could imagine how dusty it must have been, how filthy. But never mind, it turned out (though poorly, it is true).

What was our study stage comprised of? During the rehearsals for *The Great Consoler*, I reconstructed this stage in its entirety and worked on it.

There was a very small space for the audience, where benches stood in several rows. Further along, stood two columns, between which was situated the first curtain that could be parted in the middle. The wings ran along the sides. Beyond, ran a second curtain that could also be drawn back. Behind, was a backdrop, while on the sides were two rooms for props, furniture, and the actors. Behind one of the columns, unseen to the viewer, Sergei Komarov regularly stood, carrying on the most responsible work in the performance: he did the montage, and gave two students signals to open and draw the curtains, having a list of scenes, and knowing the entire étude by heart. Likewise, he gave cues to the man who switched the various lamps on and off. The lamps were arranged fairly simply: one stood to the rear, one was mounted above, and two lights were set at the sides of the main stage (half-kilowatt lamps, I think, of about 500 or 100 candlepower).

The action took place either on the front stage, or the back one. The second curtain was drawn, props and furniture were moved about behind it. The most crucial thing was the movement of things on the front stage, because we performed continuously—the curtains immediately opening and closing. What was needed was a high degree of organization, so as to have time to place all the objects. If this was a little too difficult, then we organized a scene this way: the actors stayed to perform in front of the first curtain, while during this time we were able to arrange the necessary props.

All the objects were real: armchairs, tables, and chairs, the aforementioned cubes and steps, from which various combinations of decor resulted. Apart from this, for the montage-structuring of movement and for the improvement of *mise en scène*, black velvet screens were needed to look like square columns. And this was the entire assortment of equipment for the stage. The performances were action filled, the movement structured as a form of its own, but the most interesting aspect of the spectacle for me was the movement of the equipment.

Often I did not look at the spectacle, but climbed up onto some kind of ladder and watched how the set change went, which had also been structured very exactly in all its movements, just as the rehearsed étude. The objects always stood in a certain particular place. And it was calculated how they might be best carried, so as to get them most quickly to their place. This was simply "notational" work—which things went where. It was most interesting that those students who took part in this work of set changing made a quantum leap in their acquisition of acting technique in the educational études. The organization of the set changes played an enormous educational role for students in their work on movement.

Twelve years later, I applied my system of conducting my work in these school exercises to my work on *The Great Consoler.*

Next, the following took place. I, along with those who worked with me—Pudovkin, Khokhlova, Komarov, Podobed, and others—left the school. A conflict began to grow within the school as to the proper training of actors. Two positions developed there, neither of which accommodated us. One, a particular theatrical training of actors, a training "by the *ancien régime,*" and the second, which took its root from us but which transformed the work of the film actor into a schematized, unreal, deliberate work. The conflict over these distinctions was so intense and contentious that we really needed to separate ourselves, and so we organized ourselves in the manner of an independent production collective of the Model Heroic Theater. We began to achieve success in our productions. As a part of the collective there was an educational workshop. We continued to improve and to attract new people principally to replenish the complement of actors. Barnet, who had worked in my group, left GIK with us. At that time, a great event took place in the theatrical work of Moscow: the staging by Sergei Eisenstein at the Proletkult Theater of *Enough Simplicity for Every Wise Man.* This was a significant, original performance, which produced a great influence on the further formal development of the Soviet theater. Having been acquainted at that time with Eisenstein, I was extremely interested in his work in the theater. He was very interested in my work in the cinema, and together with Alexandrov began to attend our workshop and worked on montage and the technical properties of the cinema. At that time, the following people studied in our Workshop: Lopatina (who laughs so engagingly in *The Great Consoler*); Inkizhinov, who had come from Meyerhold, and has now become a White Russian emigrant; Repnin; for a brief time, Stoller, who has just done *Copper* for Mezhrabpomfilm; Doller; Svechnikov, and others.

Komarov, Khokhlova, Pudovkin, Fogel, and Podobed were already serving as instructors.

Coterminously with the activities of the workshop, we worked daily on still photography. We shot several dozen stills daily. Each of our group had been photographed from every possible angle, from the standpoint of various *typage** possibilities and situations. From these photographs we determined each person's roles, his range of performance, his possibilities. A very interesting album was assembled, which was to have a decisive significance in the new transition to production.

Then we took up the film *The Extraordinary Adventures of Mr. West in the Land of the Bolsheviks.* This film made an enormous impression in the sense that it was one of the first Soviet films shot on a level with foreign ones. It is said that it owed them nothing in terms of its technical and artistic expressiveness (at that time our cinema was substantially below the level of foreign cinema). It is fascinating that several scenes that produced a great impression in scenario readings completely failed on the screen.

The scenario was written by myself and Pudovkin from a treatment by Aseev. Individual parts of the scenario elicited laughter while read—for example, the scene in which the bandits robbed the foreigner in full view of the Bolsheviks. They had appeared before him at night, made up as monster-Bolsheviks in sheepksins turned inside-out and armed with hammers and sickles. These scenes did not look good on the screen.

Those scenes, however, that did not raise any laughs while read, were funny on the screen. This is extremely interesting in accounting for the different effect of literature and the cinema. We still knew little about that then. The first serious lesson in the study of scenarios was with *Mr. West.*

* See Kuleshov's discussion of *typage* on pp. 63–65.

In working on *West* we developed a very interesting semi-rehearsal method. (I am considering returning to it again in coming productions, but already in an "expanded plan.") I went to the shooting set and rehearsals of *West* as the "chief observer" or "chief-in-command," while Pudovkin, Khokhlova, Obolensky, Komarov, and Podobed created sets with various decorations. Each of them separately rehearsed in the course of a day or two their assigned part of a scene or an entire scene. I went from one set to another in the studio and observed how these rehearsals progressed, and directed the work. To their most minute detail, all the scenes were staged in this manner by various people, various co-directors, various assistants, but solely under my direction. In this fashion, already with *Mr. West,* the rehearsal method was applied, but the entire work was not rehearsed in advance—rather, individual scenes were.

All the scenes that had to be shot on a given set were rehearsed a day or two in advance of the shooting. What is interesting is that the director of the studio reacted to the rehearsal almost as if to an act of sabotage. Each day one had to survive a struggle over the right to rehearse. The directress demanded that we quit the "disgrace" and "hooliganism" and the ridiculous waste of time. It is interesting to recall the conditions of the work; the studio was empty and unheated, good lighting was unavailable. The brilliant cameraman, Levitsky, who is now, sad to say, without work, did the shooting.

We shot everything under "arc" lights, that is, lights with one pair of terminals. Imagine that a pair of carbons have been removed from a lamp and that they are being used for the lighting without any reflectors. We shot the entire film with these sorts of "arcs" locked into metal boxes. That is what constituted the first lighting. The carbon holders were so inadequate that the molten carbons were forever falling, burning the floor, tables, chairs, and the costumes of the actors. This filming was also hazardous for the actors' heads, but at that time it was impossible to lessen the danger. The cameraman, Levitsky, a great artist, adaptive to situations, performed absolute miracles with the lighting. In order to make the interior lighting of the "jail set" interesting, Levitsky took only one arc, hung it in place of the imagined ceiling, found a broken section from some sort of iron gates outside the studio, tied it with ropes underneath this "arc," and the entire room was lighted with lines and patterns. This was an extremely effective shot, produced absolutely from nothing.

We introduced into the collective a particular system of rewards. For first-class disciplined work we handed out a brown button, which was worn in a buttonhole. For work in which life was risked, we gave out a red button.

Our group showed wonders of discipline. For instance, Komarov is taken in long-shot. At this moment, a great oak door flies off its hinges and smashes him over the head. Levitsky goes on shooting. We later looked at the shot frame for frame. Komarov, even though he saw that the door was falling directly on top of him, never interrupted his performance for a moment. Khokhlova went on shooting for five days with a temperature of 104°F. She had measles. Khokhlova worked the entire day while we worked in two and a half shifts, and no one thought (so difficult was it to get a set and so important was it to build it) that Khokhlova should not be involved in the shooting. We had to go on shooting no matter what happened. Sletov broke windowpanes out with his bare hands—this was the most ordinary event. Interesting from the standpoint of discipline and indicative of our work at that time was a story that involved an aerial performance between buildings, and what happened to Fogel and one particular actor (let us call him "X"). The following trick appeared in one of the films: between two five-story buildings, at the height of the fifth story, a rope was stretched—that is the way it was on the screen. One of the buildings was on one side, the second on the other, and beyond that one, yet a third. Between the first and the second—a not very large stairwell. On the roof of the stairwell was a loop (a figure eight was strung over two chimneys or two balustrades), and a rope connected to the center of the loop, the other end of which was fastened to the roof of the adjoining five-story building. This end of the rope was held by hand. According to the scenario, actor "X" was to climb across the rope from right to left suspended by his hands and legs. Later the rope was to be released and it was to start swinging between the two houses, until it stopped of its own accord. On the screen the result was as follows: the rope was released, it swung between the houses (the empty stairwell was not visible on the screen). By means of montage the actor was seen to smash into a window and to emerge in a room. I gave actor "X" his instructions to begin training, estimated how much time this would require, and the training ropes were strung in the workshop. "X" climbed up once or twice and announced: "No more is necessary. I'll do it all without any problems." During the shooting a fifteen degree (C) frost set in. "X" climbed up. So that he wouldn't smash himself up, he was "insured": he wore a leather strap on his arm, which was fastened to the main rope by a strong piece of rope. If "X" had let go with his hand, he would have remained hanging by the leather strap. This was the only possible safeguard, since any other would have been visible on the screen. "X" climbed, tired midway, hung down by his safeguard, and requested that he be removed from the rope. But he hung midway between two buildings at the height of five stories, and could not be reached in any way whatsoever. To this day, "X" has no recollection of the "flight" across. "X" was a healthy person, a fine actor, a strong and brave fellow, and this incident only took place because the actor did not seriously train himself.

Then Fogel took up the performance of this trick. He trained in the workshop some two weeks.

During the shooting, while the temperature was still freezing, Fogel needed to dangle his feet in the air, required jokes, needed to be given a cigarette, a glass of wine, etc. He repeated the aerial trick several times, performing it absolutely brilliantly from the technical standpoint. After Fogel had come down, it was revealed that the rope figure eight, on which Fogel had to swing himself, had worn through during the shooting and had been hand-held by an assistant, one Sveshnikov, while the shooting lasted some fifteen to twenty minutes. Imagine—Sveshnikov holding the rope by hand, on which a man swings over a sheer drop, and holding it in freezing weather, on a slippery rooftop. If Sveshnikov had let go the rope, Fogel would have been smashed to bits.

Incidentally, Sveshnikov, Fogel, and Sletov were our specialists in aerial work the whole time. Fogel had climbed atop one of the very highest industrial smokestacks in Moscow, strolled along its edge and did a jig. He simply had an astral sense of heights. Sveshnikov did virtually the same thing. They were absolutely festooned with red buttons. In *The Death Ray* Sletov descended by a rope from a height of about seven or eight stories. By the way, the cameraman Kuznetsov worked masterfully from heights.

After *The Extraordinary Adventures of Mr. West*, we shot *The Death Ray.* During this film, Pudovkin leaped from a four-story height, and unsuccessfully at that—smashed himself up and lay ill some two weeks (the firemen used got careless and lowered their net during his fall). This was a very original film. It was our desire to gain for ourselves the right of working and to become the very first in the cinema, the very best, and we decided to demonstrate everything we could do, no matter what the consequences. We wrote the scenario with Pudovkin, into which just about everything that could be done in films was stuffed; all the film tricks, all the film combinations, all the film situations, and of course the scenario would not work in any way at all. But we shot the film anyway. In the technical sense, this was the bill of fare of Soviet cinematrography. "Look at everything we can do. We do not lag behind the West and America at all."

At this time Eisenstein decided to do a film based on Russian revolutionary material, which was not considered photogenic enough by us at that time. We used to say: There you see a filmmaker shooting urban material—nothing is coming of it. But the reason was that the particular director was shooting city subjects poorly, not because the material was unphotogenic. Yet, it still seemed to us: "But how could revolutionary struggle, as it were, be shot in the city, when it turns out poorly . . . ?" That is how silly we were then.

Eisenstein began work on *Strike.* He depicted an episode of the revolutionary struggle of the Russian workers, and what is more the film was at cross purposes: on the one hand, it had all those excellent characteristics on which Eisenstein worked subsequently; but at the same time, the film was shot in the tradition of the theatrical grotesque, which was absolutely unsuited to the cinema, and Eisenstein realized in practice that one cannot work according to theatrical principles. Since, it seems to me, Eisenstein is a person who is extraordinarily gifted, a genius, he immediately adapted to all the laws and requirements of the cinema very easily.

The story of our period of unemployment, which lasted close to two years, follows. Because we worked as a collective with new methods, opposed to the old, theatrical film methods of Khanzhonkov and Yermoliev ("Khanzhonkovesque" and "Yermolievesque" variety), the filmmakers of the old school began to slander us, while the management, under their influence, began to fear us. (At that time, old filmmakers and prerevolutionary distributors headed the film studios.)

We were each separately offered jobs in one or the other organization, but with the provision that we should not work together. The director-distributors were especially incredibly opposed to Khokhlova.

They babbled on for a half-year, then a year, while, as far as eating was concerned, there was nothing. I stood firm, Khokhlova stood firm, several more people stood firm, while some went into independent work. Finally, I, myself, arranged jobs for some comrades, because I was regarded a definite authority by the heads of the film studios. I arranged for Pudovkin to go to "Russ." * He made a nontheatrical film there at first, and then began work on *Mother.* Komarov and Fogel were also forced to go to work at "Russ."

At long last, I began to work at the Goskino studio myself. Simultaneously with my coming, a "catastrophe" developed there—a total absence of funds, to the point of a studio shutdown. (Meanwhile, all directors required a great deal of money to shoot.) Then Viktor Shklosvky and I began to think: how to make "the most inexpensive yet artful film." From the artistic standpoint, it seemed clear to us that actors in this film would have to act according to the methods used in the étude "Gold," which we had performed in our time at the workshop. We began to search out a theme and discovered a short

* Another film studio of prerevolutionary origin. R.L.

story by Jack London called "The Unexpected," from which we both wrote a shooting scenario in one night (for thirteen hours I wrote uninterruptedly; when I rose from the table, everything was completed).

The scenario was accepted, but from habit they said that Khokhlova could not perform in it, because she was not pretty and in the cinema one must film only pretty girls, and that, as few of our collective as possible participate. I still stood my ground. The collective did film together. "Russ" lent us Komarov and Fogel for a few hours a day, as well as Galadjev and Podobed, who had worked in my collective.

How did we work on the film *By the Law*?

The film had only one set. We built it outdoors on the studio premises. Levitsky could not shoot the film, he was busy on another production, and he then talked me into beginning the work with a young novice cameraman (he had earlier been a lighting technician, then a very fine photographer, a newsman)—K. A. Kuznetsov. Beginning with this film, I worked with Kuznetsov without interruption. Kuznetsov shot *By the Law*, while Levitsky was production head. He visited us all the time and supervised the shooting. The work proceeded this way: we would shoot mornings, and the entire evening, and we would rehearse part of the night what we were going to shoot the next day, with maximal precision to the last detail, the last movement.

Thus, the rehearsal method in *By the Law* was somewhat extraordinary in character. It approached the method in *West*. All the rehearsals took place on the eve before the shooting. But the method of using assistants that had been used in *West* was not employed in this film. I staged every scene from beginning to end myself, having stopped "training assistants." But during the period of *The Death Ray* we had continued to work this way in a directorial collective. I was the head director, while Pudovkin, Komarov, Obolensky, Khokhlova were the director-assistants or co-directors. They prepared scenes according to my instructions.

One other fact needs mentioning. It is related to the new methods of working: the simultaneous staging of several films by one director, the actual realization of which I have approached this year.

After we had shot *The Death Ray*, we worked on a project for the production of a large film on the theme of "October," approximately along the same lines as the film Eisenstein was to do in the future, and simultaneously with this general film, we decided to make another four films. We worked out projects for five simultaneous productions, put together the shooting schedules and estimates. Each of these five films was to cost around 200,000 rubles. I was the chief director who was responsible for all five productions. They were planned to be shot during a period of about a year and a half. The main, general work was done by me with my co-directors—Pudovkin, Obolensky, Khokhlova, and Podobed—while the secondary productions were done by one of them under my supervision and with the assistance of the entire group. This project evolved in the actuality of production on *West* and *The Death Ray* and was turned over to Goskino, but did not get approval.

Returning to *By the Law*, it is interesting to note unexpected participation in the shooting. Suddenly, the shooting plan began to collapse for us (we shot the entire film within four months nonetheless), because we shot the set during the summer, began to make fluff from the white poplars for snow, and it became impossible to shoot on the platform. This caused us a great deal of suffering.

It is very interesting to remember how the outdoor shooting in *By the Law* took place. We had to be in time to catch the ice floes thawing in the spring. We had a house built on the shore of the snowy river bank, and this house had to be flooded with water when the ice came into contact with it. That particular year there was a flood, and the house was suddenly surrounded by a river of water. We had to be in time to shoot the scene on the ice before the on-coming ice floe, but when it was to come was uncertain. This was the most difficult task of my entire film career and the life of the collective. First, it was necessary to work on the ice all the time. The actors' hands and feet were scratched and bleeding. The actors (and, of course, the entire group) were sprayed with water from a hose the whole time, while for "wind" we ran an airplane motor. Fogel lay tied up on the snow two and a half hours. We filmed him lying on the snow, sprayed with water, in freezing weather.

We shot continuously from the onset of darkness to the onset of dawn, all evening and all night. Afterwards, everyone came to my house, fell into a heap together, soaked, often without undressing—without the strength to undress—and fell asleep. After an hour or two, we were wakened and taken by car to the outskirts of the city for shooting. That was the way we filmed for a week.

With this film the "historical" period of our work draws to a close. Later (after *Your Acquaintance*), the period of "Mezhrabpom-Russ" begins, about which I don't care to remember.

My happy "present" period, and that of my compatriots, begins with the work on *The Great Consoler*, and if we are really to learn socialistically to lend our efforts to our work, this "present" period will be full of new artistic possibilities, of new accomplishments, for us all.

[1934]

ADDRESS TO THE UNION OF SOVIET FILM WORKERS

I MUST touch on very important questions, the time is short, and I shall try to speak briefly, concisely.

I have made very many bad films. I am not going to repent that here, because, however eloquently and impassionately I might speak, no one will believe me anyway, because words are not the answer, but actions, one's work.

I am not the only one to make bad films. Bad films are made by others too. But neither I nor others have the right to work badly.

Why not? Because in the Soviet Union our directorial work is not only a matter of personal creative individuality. It is not a matter of individual talents, but it is first of all a Party matter. It is a concern of the entire revolution. It is a concern of socialism's construction. It is the concern of our whole lives.

Dovzhenko has stated that enthusiasm for work is not enough. It is not enough to feel love for the revolution. Dovzhenko stated that the base for a director's work should be knowledge, knowledge with a capital letter.

When an artist takes a stand in opposition to our way of life, our society, the most absurd, the most stupid things develop, because our way of life, our society at its core, is distinct from bourgeois life. When in our conditions an artist takes a stand opposed to actuality, this means that he opposes the whole direction of historical events—opposes the Party, its leadership, opposes the working class; in other words, he becomes absurd, ludicrous, and foolish. Therefore, in order to make good films, one must observe fundamentals, and a fundamental truth is that art must be Party oriented. A director must be a Party person from head to toe, wholeheartedly and wholemindedly. And this means first and foremost that the director must know life. He must be familiar with philosophy. He must know science and art. Knowledge characterizes the Party-oriented director. Clearly Party-oriented work cannot exist without love for the Revolution, the collective, the Party, our leadership, without a socialistic relationship to labor.

This seems to me to be most important, ought to characterize our work, and it is about this absolutely important matter that one must speak.

During the days of the Anniversary* we shall speak of the wonderful people of our cinema—about Eisenstein, about Dovzhenko—but this is not what is most important. Most important is the working class, most important is Party participation. And if we did not have an Eisenstein and a Dovzhenko, if they had not been born, the 15-year history of our cinema would have had major masters all the same. But Dovzhenko and Eisenstein as individual creators are remarkable by virtue of their being the most talented artists of the Revolution, the most talented artists of the working class.

Like other comrades, attached to a whole series of production misfortunes, I want to be among our remarkable revolutionary artists; and we will become that only when, with our flesh and blood, our entire organism, we blend with the Revolution, with Party matters. This is what is most important.

Comrade Dinamov [the previous speaker] said that what is basic in my films is the emotion of fear. Does this emotion correspond to the emotions surrounding us in our life? Above all I must comprehend

* Kuleshov was speaking of the coming celebration of the 20th year of the October Revolution, to be held in 1937. R. L.

this, and on the basis of this comprehension, on the basis of a knowledge of life, on the basis of respect and love for the working class and Party leadership, rebuild my work. But I also wish my rebuilding and my errors not to evoke ill-willed delight and general glee.

I have just made a poor film.* And due to this there is a grand celebration at our studio, one might say, a stormy celebration—"Kuleshov failed."

VOICE: That's not so.

DINAMOV: Such things do happen, comrades.

KULESHOV: I want to request, I demand, that in this rebuilding I be helped by my comrades, by the Union, by our Party organizations.

I have the right to make this demand, this is my legal demand, and I insist on it. It cannot be otherwise, because I work among Bolsheviks, and Bolsheviks know how to treat people Bolshevistically.

The purpose of my remarks is simple. It is my wish to proclaim: long live Party art, long live Bolshevik cinema! And all who can't understand this will be swept away by the wind of socialist revolution, as the tin cans are blown along in Pudovkin's film *Storm Over Asia*. Life will become merciless toward those people who are unable to follow in the footsteps of the Party. These people—perhaps even talented individuals—will be stricken from Soviet cinematography.

Unfortunately I am ill and have been unable to attend all the meetings of this conference. I listened to the report of Dovzhenko. He had made errors, but he spoke truthfully. Dovzhenko spoke of important things.

I would like to speak about the speech of Yutkevich. Yutkevich provided us with a great quantity of well-intentioned prescriptions. He gave us such a quantity of them, that it seems to me he invented the term "streamlined form"—which probably derives from the word "pharmacist." † It is not a matter of a pharmacist's precision of aim,

* *Theft of Sight*, unreleased, though officially "directed by" Leonid Obolensky, was regarded as Kuleshov's responsibility as its artistic supervisor. See "The Rehearsal Method" for references to its experiment in simultaneous production, an experiment that the Mezhrabpom Studio did not try again. R.L.

† Kuleshov's reproachful pun, directed at Sergei Yutkevich, involves an untranslatable double entendre between the Russian for "streamlined forms"—a term Yutkevich

but a matter of passion and wisdom. That is the key to our work. It seems to me a Soviet director ought to have the heart of Dovzhenko, the passion of Dovzhenko, and the wisdom of Eisenstein. These are the proper "ingredients" for a Soviet film director. (Applause)

Apropos Sergei Mikhailovich (Eisenstein), who, from this podium, with very warm, moving, tearful smiles, has been prematurely buried. A great many comrades have spoken of Sergei Mikhailovich as of a corpse. I wish to say to him as to a very live man, whom I love very much and exceptionally respect: My dear Sergei Mikhailovich! Yutkevich has said that one can burst from knowledge, and he fears that this may happen to you. Dear Sergei Mikhailovich, people burst not from knowledge, but from envy.

That's all I wanted to say. I have spoken concisely, as I had to fit it into 15 minutes.

In the corridor here I was approached with a request to clarify my position with respect to the unsuccessful work that I did with Comrade Obolensky. I can do this. The fact is that the work really did come off badly, but I am forced not to despair by the fact that the method of our work—the rehearsal method—is quite correct. And now as I ponder the film, it seems perfectly clear to me that we can reshoot one-half to two-thirds of the film. Nothing awful will happen, because the entire film was shot in two months. And if in the course of work I spend 15 to 25 days shooting—nothing grave will happen while the picture is being shot anew. Having spent only two hundred thousand plus rubles on the film, I can spend ten to fifteen thousand extra. I see the matter clearly. It is all in my hands. Talk continues about minimal means and a minimal deadline for work on the sound-stage. The most criticized part of the film is that part of the action set in Moscow. I shot in Moscow for twelve days. It is perfectly apparent that I can easily shoot that again.

---

apparently made use of during his own address preceding Kuleshov's—and the Russian for pharmacy (*obtekaemaya forma* and *apteka*). The pun refers to Yutkevich's overabundant "prescriptions" for the ailing Soviet cinema and his possibly showy use of apparent neologisms such as "streamlined form" (*obtekaemaya forma*). In Russian the two terms in question are pronounced and sound as if they might stem from the same root.

THE PRINCIPLES OF MONTAGE
(From "The Practice of Film Direction")

THE THEORY of montage in the cinema is a very important and interesting theory. It has caused great concern even to me, as one who has occupied himself with this theory, as well as to critics and filmmakers. Extremely fiery disputes flared around the theory of montage from its very inception. The theory of montage demands a particularly attentive approach and study, because montage represents the essence of cinema technique, the essence of structuring a motion picture. Having worked a long time on the theory of montage, I committed a whole series of the crudest errors. Previously, I had both concluded and written that montage was so crucial to cinematography that everything else was secondary. Despite the fact that I had done much work on the very material of motion pictures, on the shots themselves, I still placed all my emphasis on montage, perfecting the entire conception of my theoretical work on it; and here lay my deepest mistake. The fact is that film material (the selection of which is determined by the ideological tendency of the artist) is the live person working on the screen, real life filmed for the screen. This material is so variegated, so significant, and so complex that to render it by mechanical juxtaposition through "film-specifics"—by means of montage—was utterly incorrect. It is here that the political and artistic error of my past years has been. But even these works contain their positive sides. From the viewpoint of these positive aspects we can also analyze the theory of montage, because it is extremely important in the work of the film director. Since the theme of this book is the practice of film direction, I shall touch upon the theory of montage as it concerns practical work, without going deeply into theoretical analyses. I shall, however, have to provide a few historical references so that the essence of the question is clear.

Montage first began in America. Prior to the Civil War and the Revolution, montage, as a consciously expressed artistic method, was virtually unused.

We are aware that the motion picture camera photographs its surrounding reality. By means of the cinema we can observe the world. Accordingly, the cinema shows us the conduct and activities of people, existing in the reality around us. The conduct of people principally results from their class interrelationships.

Thus, photographing separate actions and the various behavior of people on film, we record the real material which surrounds us. Having recorded this material, having shot it, we can show it on the screen. But this demonstration can be accomplished by various means. Before it is possible to show the different pieces photographed in reality, it is vital to edit them, to join them to each other so that the interrelationship demonstrates the essence of the phenomena around us.

The artist's relationship to his surrounding reality, his view of the world, is not merely expressed in the entire process of shooting, but in the montage as well, in the capacity to see and to present the world around him. A variety of social encounters, a class struggle takes place in reality, and the artist's existence within a particular social class infl—ences his world-view. Artists with differing world-views each perceive the reality surrounding them differently; they see events differently, discuss them differently, show them, imagine them, and join them one to another differently.

Thus, film montage, as the entire work of filmmaking, is inextricably linked to the artist's world-view and his ideological purpose.

S. M. Eisenstein, during one of his lectures at the State Institute of Cinematography, presented a particularly vivid and interesting example of various different approaches to montage. Imagine that in a period of two or three days a series of events takes place throughout the entire world. These events are recorded by reporters, and news about them is published in various newspapers. We are aware that both capitalist and communist newspapers exist. The very same events that have taken place during the given three days are printed in both the capitalist and communist press. Even if these events are printed without commentaries, without editorial explanations and commentaries, but simply as a "dry chronicle," one's relationship to them, that is, the political world-view of the editor of the paper still determines the montage of one or another paper. In a capitalist paper all the events would be edited so that the bourgeois intention of the editor, and accordingly, of the paper, would be maximally expressed and emphasized through the character of the montage of the events, their arrangement on the newspaper page. The essential exploitativeness of the capitalist system would be clouded over in the bourgeois paper in every conceivable way, with the evils of the system concealed and the actuality embroidered. The Soviet paper is edited completely otherwise: the information about these very same events would be edited so as to illuminate the entire condition of things in the capitalist world, to reveal its essential exploitativeness, and the position of the workers as it is in reality. It can be proved, with the facts related to each other in this fashion, that the ideological sense of these facts would be differently apprehended by the reader of the paper. In the communist paper the class nature of the fact will be revealed, while in the bourgeois press this nature will be fogged over, perverted.

Thus, based on this example, it becomes clear that montage (the essence of all art) is inextricably tied to the world-view of the person who has the material at his disposal.

The account is evident to everyone. But in the beginning of my work in cinema the question of montage, the questions of aesthetic theory generally, were questions which were substantially murky for me, and I did not connect them with class interpretation, with the world-view of the artist.

In order that the development of my artistic direction, and the direction of my comrades who worked along with me, be clear, I shall describe my relationship to montage starting with the first steps on my work in film.

I began to work in the cinema in 1916. We were extremely helpless artistically at that time. The cinema was only halfway toward being an art form at that time, and, honestly speaking, it didn't really exist at all. We knew and heard nothing about montage. We only wondered about how to approach this new cinematographic art, so as to learn truly how to work with it artistically, so as to learn how to understand it seriously.

The war was still going on in 1916 and the international marketplaces were closed off to Russia. Because of this, Russian cinema began to develop quickly and independently. Swirling around the films were discussions, disputes, analyses; film gazettes and journals began to appear; in the pages of the theatrical journals a theoretical dispute emerged. The argument was whether film was an art form or not. We—the young generation of filmmakers—engaged in this dispute with the most active participation, despite the fact that we had no arguments, no evidence that film was an art. It was these disputes that led to the beginning of the genesis of the theory of montage. We developed a series of discussions and debates on the theme of montage theory, and in a few years I began the book which is titled *Art of the Cinema*. It was published still later, in 1928, and subsequently it became an example of major arguments, major studies. Because of its foundation the book was deeply erroneous.

Since we ourselves did not know how to orient ourselves in the cinema, nor what cinema was—whether it was an art form or not—we decided to direct all our attention to motion picture production. We frequented motion picture theaters and looked at everything, whatever films were on the screen, and furthermore, we did not simply look at them, but we examined them with an eye toward their class appeal.

Dividing the theaters into those in rich bourgeois neighborhoods and those of the working classes, we noticed that in the central theaters viewers' reactions to films were more reserved than in the working class theaters around the city's edge. And it was extremely important, during our investigation, for us to locate those isolated moments in a film which elicited a viewer's reactions to the particular action he is shown. It was important for us which films the viewer watched attentively, the particular moment the viewer would laugh, sigh, or groan. It was likewise important to us what was happening on the screen at that moment, how the film appeared to be made in that section, how it was constructed. Films made in different countries are differently perceived by the audience.

First of all, we divided the cinema into three basic types: the Russian film, the European, and the American. (In the European cinema at that time, films made by the Swedish firm, "Nordisk," were quite popular. This firm's films in no way resembled the European-type films, but resembled the American films much more.) When we began to compare the typically American, typically European, and typically Russian films, we noticed that they were distinctly different from one another in their construction. We noticed that in a particular sequence of a Russian film there were, say, ten to fifteen splices, ten to fifteen different set-ups. In the European film there might be twenty to thirty such set-ups (one must not forget that this description pertains to the year 1916), while in the American film there would be from eighty, sometimes upward to a hundred, separate shots.

The American films took first place in eliciting reactions from the audience; European films took second; and the Russian films, third. We became particularly intrigued by this, but in the beginning we did not understand it. Then we began to reason as follows: An argument ensues about cinema—is it or is it not an art? Let us set up a camera, actors, create decorations, play out a scene, and then let us examine the photographed segment from the viewpoint of the solution of this problem. If a good photograph results from the given piece—one which is well-shot, and beautifully and effectively conceived—then we can say: This is not cinematic art, this is merely an art of the photographer, the cameraman. If the actor performs well, we can say about the segment: Whatever the actor can do here, he also does in the theater. Where is the specificity of the cinema here? If the decor in the film is good, and the work of the designer good, then once more it can be said that there is not any cinema here: it is the work of the set designer.

However hard we tried, we could not find a fundamental, designative specificity of the art of cinema. What were we thinking about? We were thinking then about a very simple matter—every art form has two technological elements: material itself and the methods of organizing that material.

No art exists independently, by virtue of itself alone.

The problem of art is to reflect reality, to illuminate this reality with a particular idea, to prove something; and all this is only possible when one has something to evidence, and one knows how to go about it, that is, how to organize the material of the art form. Here the fact emerged that the artist, perceiving and generalizing reality, performs a definite, purposeful ideological work. Reflecting in his production an objective reality, the artist must express his ideas, demonstrate something, propagandize something: while all this is only possible when he has something to produce, and he knows how to work, that is, how the material of his art is to be organized.

In the cinema the understanding of the material and the understanding of the organization of this material are particularly complex, because the material of the cinema itself demands particular organization, demands particularly extensive and specifically cinematic treatment. The cinema is much more complicated than other forms of art, because the method of organization of its material and the material itself are especially "interdependent." Let us say, in the case of sculpture—having the fact and phenomenal appearance of reality, as well as the artistic idea, illuminating this reality with a particular object—we take a piece of marble, give it that form which is necessary for the expression of that appearance of reality, and the result is the production of a piece of sculpture. For the expression of that phenomenon in painting we take pigments and begin to organize them according to the demands of the best and most vivid expression of that phenomenon, and we get the production of a painted art work.

In the cinema the question of the constitution of a film is a far more complicated one. In the cinema, being possessed of an idea, taking the material—actual life or actors—and organizing it all by one or another method, is insufficient.

But more about this later. Thus, finding nothing in any particular segment of the film material specific to our art, consistent with the views of the time, we decided that the specifics of cinema were contained in the organization of the cinematic material (which meant separate shots and scenes), in the joining and alternation of scenes among themselves, in other words, in montage. It seemed to us at that time absolutely apparent that the American films achieved the greatest audience reactions, because they contained the greatest number of shots, from the greatest number of separate scenes, and accordingly, that montage, as the source of expression, as the artistic organization of material, affected the viewer more strongly and vividly in American films.

At that time we regarded the artistic effect of American film on the viewer very naively. The real essence of the American cinema, the real reason for its specific influence on the audience, escaped us.

But the matter, from my viewpoint, lay in the following: The flowering of American cinema was the result of the development of American capitalism. Capitalist America was being constructed, capitalist America developed, because the American society needed strong, energetic builders, fighters for the strengthening of the relics of capitalism. The Americans needed to utilize human resources at their disposal for the creation of a mighty capitalist order. This society required people of a strong bourgeois psychological orientation and world-view. Thus what was completely clear was that the task of American cinema was the education of the particular sort of person who, by virtue of his qualities, would fit in with the epoch of the development of capitalism.

At the same time capitalism inevitably nurtured the development of a proletarian class, and the consciousness of this class must have been awakening and developing; and it is utterly apparent that capitalism had to cloud this consciousness, to distract it, to weaken it. American art inevitably had to become a "consoling" art, an art that lacquered reality, an art that diverted the masses from the class struggle, from an awareness of their own class interests; and, on the other hand, it had to be an art that directed energy to competitiveness, to enterprise, larded with bourgeois morality and bourgeois psychology.

That is how the "American detective" was created—the American adventure films. From one point of view, they brought attention to energy, to competitiveness, to action; they attracted attention to the type of energetic and strong "heroes" of capitalism, in whom strength, resourcefulness, and courage were always victorious. On the other hand, these films accustomed one to bigotry, to the lacquering of reality, "consoling" and educating one to the fact that with corresponding energy a person can achieve individual fortune, can provide rent for himself, and can become a happy landowner.

The dramatic line of energy of the competition, the action and victory of those who found the strength in American films (to achieve their ends), created the rapid American montage of incidents. The American viewer demanded that directors pack the greatest amount of action into a given length of film, the greatest number of events, the greatest possible energy, pitted characters against each other more vigorously, and built the entire construction of the film more energetically and dynamically. From this point of view, from the viewpoint of the construction of rapid action montage, American cinema was a progressive "presence" at that time.

In European films, produced in those countries where the growth of capitalism was not so stormy as in America, where the American struggle for survival did not exist, there were no conditions for the genesis of a rapid, energetic montage.

Thus the structure of American films of that time, the method of their editing, was, to a certain extent, a progressive occurrence. That is how we perceived it at that particular time. We decided that the American system of montage would give us the opportunity in our

Futuristic works "to create" havoc, to break with the old world, the old petty bourgeois morality. That is where our deepest mistake lay. Perceiving the petty bourgeois axioms of American montage and American morality in their entirety, we introduced elements of bourgeois art into our own films unintentionally—a "consoling," bourgeois morality, and so on; and that is why, along with a certain benefit derived from the uncritical study of American montage, came great harm.

It seems to me that all the errors of my filmmaking during the ensuing years have their roots in this period—in the period of a blind acceptance of American film culture. This is explainable by the fact that, in our time, we were convinced that American montage invariably inculcated boldness and energy, indispensable to revolutionary struggle, to revolution.

We understood montage futuristically, but when it came to the negative aspects of its relationship to the bourgeois essence of American films, we were gulled.

I return to our "history." Studying montage we decided that in American films not only did the scenes change and alternate more rapidly than in European or Russian films, but the majority of these scenes were likewise comprised of a whole order of elements, of separate pieces, separate compositions—that is, we classified the internal division of scenes into the now universally familiar close-up, medium-shot, long-shot, and the rest. At that time this convention was new to us, and it was most important for us to have discovered it in the American cinema. We could see that in individual scenes the Americans used so-called "close-ups"—that is, that at necessary, expressive moments, they showed things in large format, more distinctly, that in a given moment, they showed only what it was necessary to show. The close-up, the compositional expression of only the most important and necessary, proved to have a decided influence on our future work in montage.

The close-up established exceptionally broad possibilities for the future montage construction of motion pictures. By means of close-ups, we arrived at the study of the potentialities of montage, we determined what it was possible to achieve through montage, how expressive its artistic strengths were . . . and a whole order of other crucial and interesting moments for our work.

We ascertained what montage would permit while simultaneously depicting lines of action in different locations.

* * *

We likewise decided that montage had an enormous influence on the semantic comprehension of what is on the screen.

Let us say that an actor is performing some sort of dismal moment; you film his drawn face. The face is shot in a setting of "dismal context." But there are instances when this face within a "dismal" scene, by virtue of its compositional properties, is found to be suitable for a cheerful scene. With the help of montage, this face could be spliced into such a scene, and instances do occur when a particular performance by an actor is given a totally different meaning through montage. I recall, even in 1916–1917, how the then famous matinee idol, Vitold Polonsky, and I had an argument about this property of montage to override the actor's performance. Emphasizing that, however one edits, the actor's work will invariably be stronger than the montage, Polonsky asserted that there would be an enormous difference between an actor's face when portraying a man sitting in jail longing for freedom and seeing an open cell door, and the expression of a person sitting in different circumstances—say, the protagonist was starving and he was shown a bowl of soup. The reaction of the actor to the soup and to the open cell door would be completely different. We then performed an experiment. We shot two such scenes, exchanged the close-ups from one scene to the other, and it became obvious that the actor's performance, his reaction of joy at the soup and joy at freedom (the open cell door) were rendered completely unnoticeable by montage. We made use of this example to emphasize that, apart from montage, nothing exists in cinema, that the work of the actor is absolutely irrelevant, that with good montage it is immaterial how he works. This was incorrect because in a particular instance we have had dealings with the poor work of an actor; and, clearly, then, these two reactions are completely different, and it is not always possible to alter the semantic work of an actor. (In certain instances the cited property of montage can be used, say, to correct an error, to change a scene, to reconstruct the scenario. It is extremely important, however, that it be possible and necessary to use this property only if there is a shooting script, a specific purpose, not in the actor's performance, but in the nature of the filming itself, in the type of face, or in the social concept.)

In this example, we taught that montage alternations are *not* only contained in the segments themselves, but in the very action that is being photographed. Imagine, if you will, that we have an alternation of segments through montage. I conceive them in terms of a line. (See Fig. 2.)

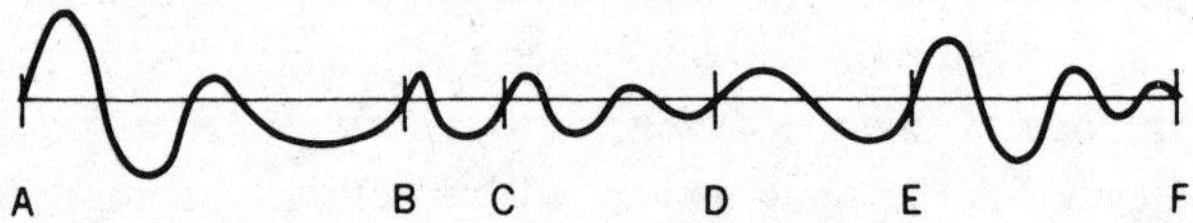

FIGURE 2. A diagram of montage segments and intra-shot montage.

There are separate marks of A, B, C, D, E, F—places marking the splices of montage segments, establishing their interrelationships, their interactions. The rhythm and meaning of the montage is not only derived from the interaction and interrelationship of the given segments marked on the line, but the montage also resides within these shots, in the filmed action of the person, for example, in the actor's performance (this internal rhythm is also apparent in the drawing of the sinusoidal curve).

Within these segments, the actor somehow conveys himself, performs some sorts of emphases through movement; his work has its own montage curve, particularly in montage interactions and alternations. It is these very alternations, in meaning as in rhythm, which are inextricably connected with the alternation of the segments themselves—that is, the internal montage of the construction of the shot cannot be separated from the entire montage construction, from the montage of the shots. But at the same time, one must not forget that the location of the shot in a montage phrase is crucial, because it is the position that, more often than not, explains the essence of the meaning intended by the artist-editor, his purpose (often the position in the montage alters the content). Let us recall the example of the bourgeois and the Soviet newspapers about which Eisenstein spoke. The interaction of separate montage segments, their position, and likewise their rhythmic duration, become the contents of the production and world-view of the artist. The very same action, the very same event, set in different places with different comparisons, "works" differently ideologically. Accordingly, a montage of segments in its turn is related to an intra-shot montage, but at the same time, the shot position in the montage is inextricably tied to the ideological purpose of direction of the editor.

It is interesting that when the director does not know his work with actors well enough, when he does not have sufficient command of the technique of this work, he tries to rectify all his errors and tries to compensate for the inadequacies of his acting with montage; and when the director constructs the basis of his picture principally on montage, he gradually loses confidence in his work with the actor. This can be tested in a particularly vivid and revealing example. One of our distinguished directors—the director Pudovkin, working in his films principally on montage construction—loses his previous ability to work with actors more and more with each new film; and Pudovkin generally always worked well with actors. In his own time he had command of acting technique, but because he often expressed ever more complex situations in his scenarios, not through the work of a living human being, but through various combinations of montage, it seems to me that gradually he began to lose the indispensable contact with the actor and the ability to direct him.

The director can always be put in a situation when it will be necessary for him to work with poor acting material, when it will be necessary to work with actor-mannequins in *typage,* when the person physically fits the role but is unable to perform as an actor. Furthermore, in films with large formats, in complex films, where there are many performing personnel, where *typage* is also important, it is inevitable that scenes are encountered in which one has to work with people who are unqualified as actors. Doubtless, the work of such an accidental actor (not an actor but a *type*) will be very poor in quality, and it is here that the role of montage, correcting and adjusting the actor's job, is highly significant. In the example of the selfsame Pudovkin, we can see how people who are utterly unable to work as actors, demonstrate what Pudovkin required, performing adequately in a whole host of scenarios and thematic situations.

We must remember once and for always that all artistic sources are fine for the achievement of a correct ideological position in a film, and that is why, when a vivid expression of an idea must be achieved through montage above all, one must work "on montage," and when an idea must be expressed through the actor's work above all, one must work "on the actor."

At all events, one must study montage, one must work on montage, because it has an extraordinary effect on the viewer.

In no case should one assume the entire matter of cinematography to be in montage. And when we conduct a brief survey of the material of cinema, because it is filmed in shots, we will see that film material is so varied, so complex, that the quality of films never depends entirely on montage. It is determined (by the way of the ideological purpose) by the material itself, especially since the material of cinema is reality itself, life itself, reflected and interpreted by the class consciousness of the artist.

[1935]

"50"
In Maloi Gnezdnikovsky Lane

IN THE Maloi Gnezdnikovsky Lane, behind an iron lattice, stands a two-story bungalow once belonging to Liazanov. That house was either bought or rented by one Cibrario di Goden, the then representative of the American motion picture firm, Trans-Atlantic. It was in this bungalow after the October Revolution that the Moscow Film Committee was first located, to be followed shortly by the Cinema Department of Narkompros,* which took charge of the entire Soviet film industry.

At the head of that organization was a Bolshevik of long standing, Dmitri Leshenko. I was invited to take charge of documentary production, and editing, and to be a director.

It so happened that all the organizations that led our Soviet film industry—Goskino, Sovkino, the Committee on Cinematography, the Ministry of Cinematography for the USSR, and so on—were and are housed in this, now greatly enlarged and expanded, building, a film center in which the original house retains what is (apart from partitioning) virtually its unaltered appearance. It is for this reason, when one must now climb some stairs past the Committee office or when one finds oneself in the conference room, that one cannot but

* The People's Commissariat of Education, the Soviet government department dealing with education and the arts, headed by Lunacharsky from 1917 to 1929. R.L.

recall the years 1918 and 1919 with particular clarity: the same familiar marble stairs and plaster ceilings are still there.

I can remember that the first business manager of the department, T. L. Levington, used to be situated in an office converted from the former bedroom of Cibrario di Goden, and that because of this there was a sumptuous bathroom adjoining the office. (Comrade Levington, a modest and earnest toiler in the service of the Soviet cinema, distinguished by her extraordinary energy, loyalty, and love of her work, was the replacement after the Civil War as the director of VGIK; she then headed the Educational Studio of VGIK, worked in the House of Friendship, and recently retired with a pension.)

A few words about Cibrario. He turned out to be a highly successful exploiter. It fell to me to read transcripts of the inquiry held, it seems to me, in an Italian court, concerning the losses connected with the swindler Cibrario di Goden's period of residence in Russia. Along with these transcripts were descriptions of di Goden's private holdings—the house, villas in various countries, dozens of private automobiles, and so on. The losses that resulted from the swindler were substantial—some inexperienced (or perhaps too "experienced") workers of the Cinema Department ordered American cameras and film through him. The order arrived on time, but what was discovered in the crates was, carefully wrapped . . . bricks.

There is no doubt that saboteurs and counterrevolutionaries found their way into the Cinema Department. In the beginning, private firms strove to protect their goods and equipment, and that is why their own people were invariably dispatched to work in this controlling organization.

"The Bolsheviks will last about two weeks," said the critics of Soviet strength. How many times did we have to hear about these "weeks," and afterwards, months, in the course of the first post-revolutionary years! (Right up to 1924 and even later.)

In our section of the committee (as I recall, the finance section), a former valet, Tyrtov, a typical Tsarist clerk, ostentatiously wearing a huge diamond ring, covered over by black adhesive plaster, managed to wheedle a job. "So that the Bolsheviks wouldn't see it," he explained (about his plastered ring).

Loyal and honest workers were indispensable to the fledgling Soviet state. And the filmmakers must be given their due—a great many people, at first simply honestly fulfilling their obligation, were discovered, who later went on to become genuine party and nonparty Bolsheviks.

The work in the Cinema Department educated me as well, an unstable youth. I found out a great deal, began to understand a great deal, learned a great deal; and the question about whom to be and for whom to work was resolved for me then and there for always.

2: On Instructions from V. I. Lenin

During the shooting sessions of those years, especially memorable are those people whom, as a director, I would send off with a cameraman, on the instructions of Vladimir Il'ich Lenin.

The Kremlin simply telephoned us when Vladimir Il'ich found it necessary, and we took off for shooting then and there.

Black Packard automobiles were dispatched for us from the Kremlin motor pool, and occasionally Lenin's private car, a Rolls Royce now in a museum.

I found documentary directing fascinating—first, one had to witness great historical events; second, documentary shooting at that time was so primitively done that I headed off in search of new methods. The documentary cameramen of that time filmed in long shots, scarcely ever approaching for close-ups; changed angles reluctantly; and tried to find the most expressive treatments of the subject matter, without considering the montage lay-out of the material.

One must note that many cameramen resisted new shooting methods. Nonetheless, such cameramen as Lemberg, Tisse, Levitsky, Yermolov, began to adopt new methods enthusiastically and started to move the camera about quickly and deftly, stopped being wary of close-ups and learned to imagine in advance the more interesting lay-outs of the shooting material.

I remember the outstanding efforts of our cameramen during the shooting of parades in Red Square. In those years there were no set-ups for documentary shooting in precisely determined places—we scrambled all over the place, selecting the most important and interesting moments, snatching close-ups, portraits, details, and so on. Documentarists stopped being lazy when they had to climb atop roofs, on electrical cable supports, and atop factory smokestacks.

During these times Dziga Vertov began working on documentaries—in the beginning, as nearly as I can recall, virtually as some sort of unit manager. Later he became intrigued with the filming, was not reluctant to learn, listened to advice, asked a great many questions, and gradually became a director, and moreover, the founder of a school of documentary cinema, which has become world famous.

I can write nothing new about him. I would only wish that his name be kept inseparable from that of Elizaveta Svilova—a skilled editor—who always remained his friend and his teacher in the area of montage.

Having begun a friendship with Vertov, I subsequently split with him, since my love was the played film,* while Vertov, in those days, felt that it had no business existing at all.

During these times I worked a great deal on reediting—making new subjects from old films, new combinations of montage. A marvelous editor, named N. Danilova, worked along with me. There was no practical purpose to the reediting—these were pure experiments, in their own way, research skills of a certain order, which taught me both to edit and to think about the laws of editing. My experimental montage studio was situated in the Film Section, in a room decorated in the Arab style (a projection room is there now), which provided my artistic adversaries an inexhaustible supply of

* Kuleshov's reference is to acted films with scenarios, montage lists, settings, etc. R.L.

jokes about the "Arabic" studies of Kuleshov. For example, during this time I created a montage experiment which became known abroad as the "Kuleshov Effect." I alternated the same shot of Mozhukhin with various other shots (a plate of soup, a girl, a child's coffin), and these shots acquired a different meaning. The discovery stunned me—so convinced was I of the enormous power of montage.

I remember the shooting of the exhumation of Sergei Radonezhsky at Zagorsk at the request of Lenin. The majority of cameramen did not want to travel there, apparently frightened. I went there in the capacity of a director, along with the cameraman, Eduard Tisse, an old photographer, and a lighting man with his apparatus.

The spiritual leaders of the highest order did the exhumation while crowds of faithful onlookers assembled. Under heavy and expensive shrouds, the coffin appeared, in which were the half-decomposed bones and wood. Newspaper shreds had been stuffed into the skull, it seems, the Russian Gazette of the end of the nineteenth century—consequently, the monks had not very long ago transgressed the inviolability of the "remains."

A second, especially memorable filming session, particulary of this very period, was the journey across the Tverskoi province with the revision of the VTsIK.* The shooting was conducted as before, under the immediate directions of V. I. Lenin. During the time of the journey we, the cameraman Lemberg and I, not only had to shoot the film but also had to write articles in the local papers, to assist the Inspectors. It must be mentioned that documentary filmmakers nearly always fulfilled some specified mission quite apart from their regular responsibilities. Thus, Eduard Tisse was "the authorized representative of the VTsIK in the supervision of partisan combat on the Czech occupied territory." And this territory at one time stretched from the Volga to Enisei.

He was designated the head of the division of partisans by one of the directives. Another document, under the signature of Comrade Budenny attested that important papers were entrusted to him for delivery from the front to Moscow.

* Central Executive Committee of the Congress of Soviets from 1918 to 1937.R.L.

It was necessary to travel along the Volga with the revision of the VTsIK, toward the cities of Kalyazin and Kashin. In those days neither the Moscow canal nor the Rybin Sea existed, and the Volga ran shallow in places; and therefore all the passengers (including us) climbed out of the boat and pushed the boat off the shoals, whenever it ran aground, like an automobile pushed from mud onto dry land. Unfortunately, we were never able to film this scene: invariably, the boat ran aground only at night.

During this trip we shot a played (scripted and acted) documentary—the life of a camp for young criminals. The camp cast an intense impression over us of some sort of extraordinary concrete example of the government's concern for humanity. We shot right in the camp, while the fellows were unintimidated enough to play out for us a "page" of their former "activities." The documentary, beautifully shot by A. Lemberg, turned out very interesting, lifelike, and convincing.

Somewhere during this particular trip our attention was drawn to a little factory, which had been opened through the efforts of the workers themselves. Look at the preserved photograph to see how modest the production methods of this provincial factory were. But, in all honesty, somewhere there, in the depths of our hearts and minds, apparently an inkling of the coming giant results of socialism had arisen—because in fact we leaped at the chance to film this miniature but at least our own, Soviet enterprise.

In the summer of 1919 the Committee on Cinema, as far as it is known to me, likewise acting on the orders of Vladimir Il'ich, dispatched me and the cameraman, Eduard Tisse, to the Eastern Front.

Tisse and I found ourselves at the front during the Red Army's expulsion of Kolchak from Orenburg.

Normal life had already resumed in the city, but Kolchak's forces stood on the other side of the river.

We received orders to film the advance on Dongusk station (within seven kilometers of Orenburg). At first we had to shoot from an armored car, but this proved to be awkward, and Tisse and I set off in an open truck.

I remember the early morning, I remember how we crossed a bridge and were strafed by machine gun bullets in our first village. But there was nothing to film. Later we drove straight across the steppe searching after things to shoot and accidentally found ourselves within a hundred or two hundred paces of a Cossack cannon. The machine, as so often happens in circumstances such as this, stalled. The driver tried to start it up, while the Cossacks started to fire point blank at the truck.

It was at this point that I realized what a resourceful and brave cameraman was: Tisse slung his heavy (not a lightweight documentary camera) camera off the tripod in an instant, tucked it close to his chest with one arm, while continuing to crank the other camera with his free hand, and managed to photograph several shells exploding, which had been directed at us. (All this turned out beautifully on the screen.)

In a few moments, one of the commanding officers rode up to us in a light automobile and carried us away. Now we sped off again across the whole steppe (the steppe near Orenburg is as smooth as asphalt) and came under rifle fire. The driver braked the truck; the harsh voice of the commanding officer boomed, reinforced by a revolver pointed at the driver (he was a coward), and we moved off once more in the direction of the gunfire. Apparently, the officer was convinced that we were nearing the Red Army, and they were firing at us in error, having taken us for White Cossacks.

We came up to the line of soldiers; the shooting stopped, and from a distance I could see the red stars on the caps of the soldiers. The officer appeared to be right. How precious, familiar, and vivid these Red Army stars, dusty as they were from combat, became to us!

(Earlier I was able to witness the remarkable tenacity and courage of another documentary cameraman—P. Novitsky. During the filming of the exploding artillery warehouses at Khoroshov, blown up by White Army spies, P. Novitsky calmly went on shooting under a shower of cinders, changing set-ups, finding better angles, and fatefully remained unscathed.)

After the filming of combat incidents below Orenburg, Tisse and I shot footage of the Ural home front in some detail, the scars of battle, the factories of Elatoust, Yekaterinburg, the countryside around the Urals, the movement of transport, and the restoration of a new life after the retreat of Kolchak.

At Yekaterinburg, I met a youth in the Red Army, who had volunteered for the front. This was Leonid Obolensky. We spoke about the cinema. As a result, Obolensky was dispatched on orders to Moscow, with my letter of recommendation to V. Gardin—for enrollment in the Film School. For his part, Obolensky became a lifelong friend to Eisenstein and myself. At the present time he is working at the Chelyabinsk television station.

The film, *Ural*, came out beautifully; it was well received and was sold by the Committee to America for 2000 meters of raw stock; but the Americans cheated us—they shipped not 2000 meters, but 2000 feet.

3: The First Film School Through the Eyes of a Pedagogue

The first state film school was established in Moscow in 1919 (later to be called VGIK). From this point forward my fate is inextricably linked to pedagogical work.

The man who performed an especially great function in the organization of the school was Vladimir Rostislavovich Gardin; also, the chairman of the Film Division, D. Leschenko. The People's Commissar of Education, Anatoli Vasil'evich Lunacharsky, was a great friend of the school and responded to its needs with exceptional attention, often even taking part in its daily work. Apart from Gardin, L. Leonidov, O. Preobrezhanskaya, and the actor I. Khudolev taught there.

The organization of the school constituted a great many large and interesting tasks—a new, revolutionary cinema had to be born, which would sweep away all the traditions of salon cinematography with its ersatz-psychological dramas, with its sugary-sentimental "kings" and "queens" of the screen.

In 1919, having returned from the front, I began to attend the school as a guest; it was extremely interesting to me to observe the instruction.

The composition of the students of the school was very mixed in the beginning: along with talented young people, truly dreaming about working in a revolutionary film-art, adventurers, former "human beings," and bourgeois ladies came to school—the school took the place of work conscription. The former millionaire and horse breeder, Polyakov, and a "lady of the world," Nastya-Naturshchitsa—the wife of the manager of dozens of ready-to-wear dress shops, Mandel, and the mistress of the great Count Dmitri (who had slain Rasputin)—both settled into the school.

But people of Polyakov's and Nastya-Naturshchitsa's stripe did not last long at the school: some emigrated, others were arrested by the security police.

Other documentary film workers came to the school along with me, principally cameramen. In the lessons dealing with plastic instruction, they directed my attention to a tall, smoothly moving woman, leaping about in an orange robe, in a ring-dance with a group of young men and women. Because of her thinness the cameramen called her "the galloping plague"—this was A. S. Khokhlova.

Thus, at the inception of the school I was only a "sideline observer," but one day I observed a group of extremely despondent students—they had flunked their round of examinations. I offered them the opportunity to rehearse an étude with me for their reexamination.

To my surprise, the students took up my offer, despite the fact that a twenty-year-old youth with a tattered, cocked hat on his head did not much resemble an experienced filmmaker and should not have elicited, from their point of view, any particular confidence.

Having begun to work with the students, I sought to assign them études, as I saw fitting, that is, ones totally antithetical to the instruction they had received. The instructors expected of them so-called "emotionalizing": slow movement, bulged-out eyes, all manner of anguished expressions and sighs—a veritable assortment of conventions of the deposed "kings" and "queens" of the screen. For my part I attempted to construct études based on action, on physical struggle, on movement; and when it came to the stressful moments of "emotionalizing"—internalized performance—I justified them and, most importantly, connected them to the action of real life.

Everything that I was fortunate enough to have done with those students who had failed their exams was so different from the established conventions of the prerevolutionary cinema that at the reexamination the "last became the first"—they received top marks and joined the ranks of the most successful students.

After such a debut I was invited to become an instructor at the First State Film School and became a pedagogue.

Somehow, one evening, I was told during a lesson that a couple of students had staged a very amusing parody of one of the excerpts that I had staged. I asked that the work be shown to me, and what I saw really was marvelous and talented. With the sharpest irony, whimsically and wittily, with extraordinary rhythm and precision, the students had hyperbolized my "production." This was done by Alexandra Khokhlova and her partner, A. Raikh.

The first of May 1920 was upon us. This day will remain in my memory for life.

In the morning, with one of the cameramen (I don't remember with whom), my students and I were filming the documentary *The All-Russia Subbotnik*—the renovation of steam engines. During the daytime we had shot footage of V.I. Lenin at the stone-laying ceremony of the monument to Karl Marx and "Liberated Labor." Before this, Levitsky was shooting footage of the *subbotnik* at the Kremlin, but without me and my pupils. Khokhlova will describe the details of *The All-Russia Subbotnik*. (In his memoirs A. A. Levitsky does not remember our joint filming of Lenin at the stone-laying ceremony of the monument on the first of May 1920—I don't understand how he could have forgotten such a fact.)

A bit later, the first evening of screenings of the State School of Cinematography was arranged in the presence of Anatoli Vas'ilevich Lunacharsky.

One of the "highlights" of the program was the parody performed by Khokhlova and Raikh.

From that day forward Khokhlova and I worked together virtually always. (I must convey a secret—that after many years had slipped by, Khokhlova admitted that the parody she had done was in utter seriousness.)

In order to describe those first days of the film school, it is crucial to remember what the conditions of life were in 1918–1920.

This was an arduous period in the Soviet Union. There was a shortage of bread, there was no meat, no milk. Each citizen of Moscow and Petrograd (now Leningrad) was rationed to an eighth of a loaf of bread. Factories shut down or virtually shut down. There was insufficient raw material and fuel.

During the years of the genesis of the First State Film School, it was impossible to imagine the future VGIK—a center of research thinking, a center of the study and education of Soviet and international film directors, actors, cameramen, scenarists, film scholars, artists, economists.

But we were not despondent, did not become crestfallen, and deeply, sincerely believed in the triumph of Soviet governance and, therefore, in the triumph of our cinematography and our film school. (I was very anxious, remembering all this on November 22, 1965, when the great honor was bestowed upon me to inaugurate the opening of the First Conference of the Union of Cinematographers of the USSR in the Grand Palace of Congresses in the Kremlin.)

I remember one of the film factories abandoned by its owner in the winter, I think, of 1919: amidst the ramshackle buildings remnant pieces of broken furniture stood in the snowbanks, while on top of a table, peeking from underneath a layer of snow was a rusting typewriter with a sheet of paper left in its roller. This is what the "technical basis" of Soviet artistic cinematography amounted to in the days of its establishment!

The "technical basis" of the school was similar, in fact, it was nonexistent. For a long time the school did not have its own building, the curriculum was a single one—an actor's curriculum; the student body numbered about sixty.

And both the students and teachers of the school were poorly dressed for the most part, thin, chronically hungry. The school was not heated. It was no better at home. I remember that somehow we were lucky enough to heat the room with an electric rheostat: it stood on the floor, and starved mice would scuttle up to it, together with humans, not paying any attention to the people at all.

Along the streets, directly on the houses, Futurists hung their paintings. I recall that on one of the revolutionary holidays all the leaves of the trees on one street were entirely painted blue; I remember "The windows of ROST'," * Mayakovsky himself; I remember an "agit-showcase" on Tverskoi Street, under the glass of which was a piece of human skin, peeled off by foreign interventionists from the hand of a living Red Army soldier.

But however difficult it was during this period, we shall never forget the wonderful days of the twenties:

From a battle to your job—
                    from work
                              to the attack,—
In hunger,
      frost
         naked
they held
      the taken,
            yes, so it was
that blood
      came from under your fingernails. . . .

[1967]

* An acronym for the Soviet Telegraph Agency (later TASS), for which Mayakovsky created numerous posters and slogans, exhibited in the building's showcase windows. R.L.

ON THE RED FRONT

IN 1920 it fell to our workshop, which was called "The Kuleshov Workshop," to create one of the first Soviet agit-films, *On the Red Front*. This film, of an agitational, military, adventure nature, which was staged by us on the Southern front of the Civil War, in the thick of wartime action, was shot as a newsreel. The newsreel fits into the action organically. The cameraman on the film was Pyotr Ermolov.

We had to shoot the film on positive (reversal) stock (negative stock was unavailable in the country by this time), and the film was printed on primitive film stock. Despite it all, the photography, thanks to P. V. Ermolov, was extraordinary.

Actors from our workshop performed in the midst of Red Army soldiers. At times they would emerge next to the commander, Popov, who "played" himself, and, it must be said, blended with the actual background. How this was accomplished is discussed elsewhere by L. Obolensky, now working in the Chelyabinsk television station.

The completed film, released by the cinema section of the subsection for the Arts of MONO (the Moscow Division of Public Training, People's Commissariat for Education), was seen by V. Lenin, and from what we were told, he praised it.

The secret here lay in the system of training in the workshop of the actor-mannequins. The term "mannequin" was subject to the most bitter attacks, but the matter is never in a term, but in its substance. World cinema of the 1960s strives for the more lifelike in the conduct of actors on the screen, for the "real person" in a film. We also strove toward this end, not training "traditional" actors but "actor-mannequins."

L. Obolensky described this very clearly in one of his letters. He writes: "Kuleshov and I met in the Urals at the time of the easing of action on the front. The armies of Kolchak were retreating, the mood of the youth was rising. Dreams of the future were already becoming real. Kuleshov directed my dreams toward the cinema: We must build a new cinema, without theatrical dramas and beautiful poses. . . . Now we must shoot newsreels, because events are significant and cannot be duplicated. And later . . . later, in Moscow . . . there is a school, which prepares young filmmaker 'actor-mannequins'—not actors, because the cinema needs nature herself, life itself. This is not the theater, recorded on celluloid."

Thus we can see from this letter, that the "actor-mannequin" is not an obedient mannequin in the hands of the film director, as even some contemporary film scholars interpret this term. The actor-mannequin is a natural, real person, as in life, but one who is able to do anything.* He is higher and more complete than the theatrical actor. That is the actual sense of this term.

The film *On the Red Front* is not preserved. Now, in the interim of 47 years, we have been fortunate enough to find its shot-list, recorded by A. S. Kohkhlova. We analyzed it.

One must either remember or imagine the epoch during which the film was shot. This was the time of obvious propaganda, a time of "The Windows of Rost'" of Mayakovsky. This was a time when, along the streets of Moscow, it was often possible to encounter people riddled by hunger and disease. I have already written that I remember how, at that time on Tversky Street, in a glass-enclosed frame, the skin taken from the hand of a living Red Army soldier had been hung. Understand this time, and then you will understand the form and language of the first "agit-film."

* For Kuleshov the trained actor-mannequin would appear to embody no less than the set of all potential, possible human action. R.L.

In light of the shot-list of the film, it becomes clear how organically the work of the "actor-mannequins" was woven into the action.

There were two parts to the film—approximately 600–650 meters. They comprised 331 shots—so "flowing" was the montage. In the original, instead of the word tank, "tanka" *—that's how it was said then.

The actor-mannequins in the film were:

L. Obolensky—Red Army communist
A. Raikh (also a student of the film school)—a White-Polish spy
L. Kuleshov—a Polish worker
A. Khokhlova—the wife of a Polish worker
Popov—a Red Army officer

In the shot-list, the Red Army soldier, the spy, the worker, etc. were named after the persons themselves—that's how it often was in those days. All the shots with the abovementioned "actor-mannequins"—as the "chase," the furnishings of the train, the fight scene on the roof of one of the wagons, etc.—were shot on location. (Often the "acted" sequences were canceled because the Red Army was suddenly called to the front lines owing to a battle alarm.) The automobiles in the film were directed from the train by the commander of the Southern front, M. Tukhachevsky.

All the remaining shots (the majority) were a detailed newsreel of war action or frontline life.

[1968]

* In English, the analogous distinction might be between the "older" and the "modern" terms *aeroplane* and *airplane*. R.L.

BIBLIOGRAPHY
of Works by Lev Kuleshov

Books

Iskusstvo Kino: My Experience. Moscow: Tea-Kino Pechat', 1929. ("Art of the Cinema" in this volume)

The Rehearsal Method in Cinema. Moscow: Kinofotoizdat, 1935.

The Practice of Film Direction. Moscow: Goslitizdat, 1935.

The Fundamentals of Film Direction. Moscow: Goskinofotoizdat, 1941.

The Shot and Montage. Moscow: Iskusstvo, 1961.

First Films: Work with the Actor. Moscow: Iskusstvo, 1962.

The ABC's of Film Direction. Unpublished.

"*50*. Unpublished memoirs written with A. S. Khokhlova.

Articles

1917

"On the Problems of an Artist in the Cinema," *Vestnik Kinematografii*, No. 126.

"On Scenarios," *Vestnik Kinematografii*, No. 127.

1918

"The Art of Creating with Light: Foundations of Thought," *Kino-Gazeta*, No. 12, pp. 1–2.

1922

"Art, Contemporary Life, and Cinematography," *Kino-fot*, No. 1, p. 2.

"Chamber Cinematography," *Kino-fot,* No. 11, p. 3.
"Montage: From a Book on Cinematography," *Kino-fot,* No. 3, pp. 11–12.
"If Only Now . . . ," *Kino-fot,* No. 3, pp. 4–5. (Including "Chaplin's Style.")
"Artistic Cinematography," *Ermitazh,* No. 11, p. 16.
"The Film Actor-Mannequin," *Zrelischa,* No. 1, p. 16.
"Cinematography as the Fixation of Theatrical Action," *Ermitazh,* No. 13, p. 15.
"Americanitis," *Kino-fot,* No. 1, pp. 14–15.

1923
"How Our Workshop Came To Be," *Kino* (September), p. 30.
"Conrad Veidt," *Kino-Gazeta,* No. 7, p. 17.
"The Hearts of Three," *Khudozhestvennyi Trud,* No. 3, pp. 71–76.
"What Is To Be Done?" *Kino-Gazeta,* No. 3, p. 1.

1924
"Mister West," *Zrelischa,* No. 79, p. 14.
"Our Milieu and Americanism," *Kino-Gazeta,* Nos. 17, 18, pp. 33–34.
"A Straight Path," *Kino-Gazeta,* No. 48, p. 2.
"Directors on Themselves," *Kino-Gazeta,* No. 10, p. 1.

1925
"The Autocharacteristics of the Creative Method," *Sovetskii Ekran,* No. 23, p. 9.
"Will . . . Tenactiy . . . Eye," in Belenson, *The Cinema Today,* Moscow (published by the author), pp. 9–12.
"From Experimental-pedagogical Work to *The Death Ray,*" *Kino-Jurnal ARK,* No. 1, p. 24.
"The Artist in Cinema," *Sovetskii Ekran,* No. 29, pp. 6–7.

1926
"*West-Ray-By the Law,*" Kino-Gazeta, No. 36, pp. 2–3.
"One Ought to Remember," *Kino-Gazeta,* No. 9, p. 3.
"Why I Am Not Working," *Kino,* No. 10, p. 3.
"The Present Day," *Kino-Jurnal ARK,* No. 1, pp. 27–28.
"A Wheel of Traits," *Kino,* No. 11, p. 3.
"Fairbanks-Dear," *Kino,* No. 4, p. 1.
"How To Train a New Film Worker," *Komsomol'skaya Pravda,* No. 290, p. 3.
"Handiwork," *Sovetskii Ekran,* No. 11, p. 6.
"Will . . . Tenacity . . . Eye," in *Eizenshtein: Bronenosets Potemkin* (Moscow), pp. 9–12.

1927
"On the Threshold of Soviet Comedy," *Kino,* No. 16, p. 3.
"For Ten Years," *Kino,* No. 45, p. 4.
"The Screen Today," *Novyi Lef* (April), pp. 31–34.
"Of Our Film Actor," *Kino,* No. 21, p. 3.

1928
"My First Films," *Sovetskii Ekran,* No. 46, pp. 8–9.
"Our History: Photograph-études from the Works of the Kuleshov Collective," *Sovetskii Ekran,* No. 47, pp. 6–7.
"On the Theatrical Actor in Cinema," *Kino,* No. 28, p. 4.
"Notes on Film Art," *Sovetskii Ekran,* No. 24, p. 5. (Including the essay "David Griffith and Charlie Chaplin.")
"Why Was the War So Badly Filmed?" *Sovetskii Ekran,* No. 30, p. 5.

1929
"At the Sources of Soviet Cinema," *Kino,* No. 45, p. 2.
"The Wonders of Montage," *Kino,* No. 26, p. 2.
"We and the Foreign Countries," *Sovetskii Ekran,* No. 9, p. 3.
"From *West* to *Canary,*" *Sovetskii Ekran,* No. 11, pp. 6–7.
"Fogel, the Life of Art," *Kino,* No. 24, p. 2.

1930
"What Is To Be Done," *Kino I Kul'tura,* No. 11–12, pp. 18–25.

1932
"To Achieve an Improvement," *Kino,* No. 47, p. 3.
"Forgotten People," *Kino,* No. 30, p. 3.
"The Creative Impulse," *Kino,* No. 23, p. 1.
"The Creative Path of the Cameraman Kuznetsov," *Kino,* No. 27, p. 3.

1933
"The Practice of the Rehearsed Film," *Sovetskoe Kino* (December), pp. 37–43.

1934
"Two Films at Once," *Rabis,* No. 3, pp. 33–34.
"The Rehearsal Method," *Sovetskoe Kino,* No. 3, pp. 82–86.
"Our First Experiences," *Sovetskoe Kino* (November–December), pp. 126–137.

1935
"The Path of Cinema," *Vechernyaya Moskva,* No. 9, p. 3.

"Writer-Scenarist," *Literaturnaya Gazeta,* No. 3, p. 2.

"Address Before the All-Union Conference on Creativity of the Workers of Soviet Cinematography." In *Za Bol'shoe Kinoiskusstvo,* pp. 118–121. Moscow: Kinofotoizdat, 1935.

1939

"A Pretended Rehearsal," *Kino,* No. 47, p. 2.

1940

"Twenty Years," *Iskusstvo Kino,* No. 3. (A remembrance of the first twenty years of VGIK.)

1941

"The Culture of Directorial Creativity," *Iskusstvo Kino,* No. 3.

1944

"A Few Words on Rear-Projection." In *Experience in the Use of Rear-Projection Filming*. Address to conference on "Fictional Film in the Days of the Great Patriotic War."

1946

"How I Became a Director." In *How I Became a Director,* pp. 156–162. Moscow: Goskinoizdat, 1946.

1949

"Mastering the Victorious Theory of Marxism-Leninism," *Sovetskoe Iskusstvo,* No. 21, p. 1.

1960

"From the Viewpoint of a Filmmaker," *Sovetskaya Kul'tura* (February).

1962

"Five Photographs from The Archives," *Sovetskii Ekran,* No. 12, pp. 18–19.

1965

"The Unforgettable," *Put' k Ekrany* (April).

"Our Film School," *Sovetskaya Kul'tura* (November).

"Address Before the First Constituent Conference of the Union of the Cinematographers of the USSR with an Introductory Word by the Honored Worker in the Arts of the RSFSR, Professor Lev Kuleshov,"

Izvestia, November 23. (Also simultaneously published in *Sovetskaya Kul'tura* and *Pravda,* both November 24.)

"For an Art of Great Ideas and Discoveries," *Pravda,* November 24.

1967

"50" (from the forthcoming Kuleshov-Khokhlova memoirs), *Iskusstvo Kino,* No. 6, pp. 14–20.

"50" (from the forthcoming Kuleshov-Khokhlova memoirs), *Iskusstvo Kino,* No. 10, pp. 33–40.

1968

"On the Red Front" (from the forthcoming Kuleshov-Khokhlova memoirs), *Iskusstvo Kino,* No. 2, pp. 9–10.

1969

"The Great Consoler" (from the forthcoming Kuleshov-Khokhlova memoirs), *Iskusstvo Kino,* No. 1, pp. 110–117.

"Pupil and Teacher," *Nedelya* (magazine supplement to weekend edition of *Izvestya*), No. 5 (465), p. 9.

FILMOGRAPHY
of Films by Lev Kuleshov

1917

The Alarm (Nabat). 7 reels. Khanzhonkov Studio. Director: Evgeni Bauer. Designer: Lev Kuleshov.

The King of Paris (Korol' Parizha). Khanzhonkov Studio. Director: Evgeni Bauer. Designer: Lev Kuleshov.

1918

The Widow (Vdova). Khanzhonkov Studio. Designer: Lev Kuleshov.

Boulevard Slush (Sliakot' Bulvarnaya). Khanzhonkov Studio. Designer: Lev Kuleshov.

Engineer Prite's Project (Prockt inzhenera Praita). Khanzhonkov Studio. Director: Lev Kuleshov.

The Unfinished Love Song (Pesn' lyubvi nedopetaya). Khanzhonkov Studio. Co-director: with Vitold Polonsky, Lev Kuleshov.

1919

The Daredevil (Cmelchak). Neptune Studio. Supervisor: with Vladimir Gardin, Lev Kuleshov.

1919–1920

Newsreels, on Kolchak's front, Tverskaya gubernya. Newsreel of Lenin.

1920

On the Red Front (Na krasnom fronte). Kino Section, Moscow Soviet and VFKO. Scenarist and Director: Lev Kuleshov.

Filmography of Films by Kuleshov

1922
Mineral Waters of the Caucasus (Kavkazskiye mineral'nye vody). Mezhrabpom-Russ. Director: Lev Kuleshov.

1923–1924
The Extraordinary Adventures of Mr. West in the Land of the Bolsheviks (Neobychainye priklucheniya mistera Vesta v strane bolshevikov). Goskino Studio. Director: Lev Kuleshov.

1925
The Death Ray (Luch smerti). Goskino Studio. Director: Lev Kuleshov.

1926
zby the Law (Po zakonu). Goskino Studio. Co-scenarist: with Viktor Shklovsky, Lev Kuleshov. Director: Lev Kuleshov.

1927
Your Acquaintance, also *The Female Journalist* (Vasha znakomaya). Sovkino Studio. Director: Lev Kuleshov.

1927–1928
Steam Engine No. B-1000 (Paravoz No. B-1000). Goskinprom Studio. Director: Lev Kuleshov. (Unfinished)

1929
The Great Buldis (Dva-Bul'di-Dva). Mezhrabpomfilm Studio. Director: Lev Kuleshov.

1929–1930
Sasha (Sasha). Belgoskino Studio. Co-scenarist: with Leonid Obolensky and Alexandra Khokhlova, Lev Kuleshov.

1930
The Breakthrough (Proryv). Mezhrabpomfilm Studio. Director: Lev Kuleshov.

1930–1931
Forty Hearts (Sorok serdets). Director: Lev Kuleshov.

1932
Horizon (Gorizont). Mezhrabpomfilm Studio. Co-scenarist: with Shklovsky and G. Mundblit, Lev Kuleshov. Director: Lev Kuleshov.

Filmography of Films by Kuleshov

1933

The Great Consoler (Velikii uteshytel'). Mezhrabpomfilm Studio. Co-scenarist: with Alexander Kurs, Lev Kuleshov. Designer: Lev Kuleshov. Director: Lev Kuleshov.

1934–1935

Theft of Sight (Krazha zreniya). Mezhrabpomfilm Studio. Art director and production supervisor: Lev Kuleshov. Co-director: with Leonid Obolensky, Lev Kuleshov. (Unfinished)

1935–1926

Dokhunda. Tadzhikfilm Studio. Scenarist and director: Lev Kuleshov. (Unfinished)

1940

The Siberians (Sibiriki). Soyuzdetfilm Studio. Director: Lev Kuleshov.

1942

The Oath of Timur (Klyatva Timura). Director: Lev Kuleshov.

The Young Partisans (Yunye Partizany). Stalinabad Studio. Director: Lev Kuleshov.

1943

We Are from the Urals (My c Urala). Soyuzdetfilm Studio. Director: Lev Kuleshov.

INDEX

Index